God's Covering

About Ellel Ministries

Our Vision
Ellel Ministries is a non-denominational Christian Mission Organization with a vision to resource and equip the Church by welcoming people, teaching them about the Kingdom of God and healing those in need (Luke 9:11).

Our Mission
Our mission is to fulfill the above vision throughout the world, as God opens the doors, in accordance with the Great Commission of Jesus and the calling of the Church to proclaim the Kingdom of God by preaching the good news, healing the broken-hearted and setting the captives free. We are, therefore, committed to evangelism, healing, deliverance, discipleship and training. The particular scriptures on which our mission is founded are Isaiah 61:1–7; Matthew 28:18–20; Luke 9:1–2; 9:11; Ephesians 4:12; 2 Timothy 2:2.

Our Basis of Faith
God is a Trinity. God the Father loves all people. God the Son, Jesus Christ, is Savior and Healer, Lord and King. God the Holy Spirit indwells Christians and imparts the dynamic power by which they are enabled to continue Christ's ministry. The Bible is the divinely inspired authority in matters of faith, doctrine and conduct, and is the basis for teaching.

For more information
Please visit our website at www.ellelministries.org for full up-to-date information about the world-wide work of Ellel Ministries.

ELLEL MINISTRIES
TRUTH AND FREEDOM SERIES

God's Covering

A Place of Healing

David Cross

Sovereign World

Sovereign World Ltd
PO Box 784
Ellel
Lancaster LA1 9DA
England

ISBN 978-1-85240-485-7

The publishers aim to produce books which will help to extend and build up
the Kingdom of God. We do not necessarily agree with every view expressed
by the authors, or with every interpretation of Scripture expressed. We expect
readers to make their own judgement in the light of their understanding of
God's Word and in an attitude of Christian love and fellowship.

Cover design by Andy Taylor
Typeset by CRB Associates, Reepham, Norfolk
Printed in Malta

To a precious family:
Denise, Douglas, Ellen and Emily.

May we increasingly know what it means to be in Christ Jesus.

Thank you to those who have helped
to get these thoughts on paper:
Paul, Liz, Brenda and Grace.

Contents

Introduction

Wherever we see a parent enfolding a child in their loving arms, something in us says *"yes"* because it seems so right. In the same way, each one of us has been designed by God to know the fullness of *His* embrace and *His* spiritual covering. Without that covering we cannot truly be at peace. Many people are carrying the damage of spiritual exposure, from situations both past and present. Understanding God's covering is an important step to discovering His healing.

It has been a common sight at conferences to see Peter Horrobin, the director of Ellel Ministries, open up an umbrella on the stage. His purpose is to show how God covers and protects His people through godly leadership. Peter explains that, when those in leadership sin, it is like piercing the fabric of an umbrella. People sheltering under an umbrella with holes get wet. In the same way, people sheltering under an inadequate spiritual covering from leaders find that they are spiritually exposed in the areas where those leaders have sinned. As a result those sheltering become wounded and are sometimes drawn into similar sin themselves.

God's desire to cover us is not so much a decision which He has made, but an expression of His character. The subject of covering permeates the whole of the Bible in an amazing way. It is a principle which not only helps to explain the reason for so many of the problems we have, but also gives us more understanding of God's wonderful plan for restoration. God's covering provides the spiritual protection which is so essential for us, and it gives a safe place for His work of wholeness and freedom to be fulfilled in our lives.

This book seeks to explain the very damaging effect of spiritual exposure, when we are out of God's order, and the inevitable consequence of this on our health and well-being. Thankfully, there is also a precious truth of God's covenant plan for the *re-covering* of damaged lives through Jesus. In fact, I could have entitled this book *God's Recovery Service!* You can have greater confidence in praying for yourself or for others as you find a growing assurance of God's unwavering desire to re-cover you, where there has been sin, wounding and exposure.

In the story of the Good Samaritan we are told of an unsuspecting traveler who was attacked, stripped, beaten and robbed and who was only recovered from the side of the road by the one who had the true character of Jesus. Life is full of bad decisions and bad experiences in which we have found ourselves stripped of God's spiritual covering and robbed of peace. Today, like the Good Samaritan, God is ready, willing and able to pick up the pieces of our lives and take us to a place of safety and healing, where all the expenses have been paid!

In this book we are going to take a look at this principle of God's protective covering, seeking to answer these questions:

- What is it?
- What good is it to us?
- How did we lose it?
- How do we get it back?

The first eight chapters describe what covering is and how lack of covering causes problems for us. Chapters 9 and 10 talk about the solution, with prayers which I hope you will find useful. At the end of each chapter there is a summary.

CHAPTER 1

What is God's covering?

Getting the picture

What do we mean by "covering"?

"God's covering" is an expression which describes the spiritual protection and nurture which God provides for all those who are in a covenant relationship with Him. You cannot see His covering but you can certainly experience its effect. Without Jesus, the world cannot truly understand God's covering but all of mankind desperately needs it! Outside this shelter, men and women are vulnerable to a hostile spiritual realm which governs all those who remain in rebellion to the One who created them. Where God covers there is light, truth and healing. Where the enemy covers any part of our lives there is darkness, deception and damage.

God has put within the heart of every human being the desire, often unconscious, to find a place of covering. Our heavenly Father wants us to find that protection in Him. Unfortunately most people in the world, while seeing something of the relevance of covering, choose to remain dependent on their own wisdom. In fact, we often mention the subject in our conversations, with comments such as:

- Don't worry, I've got it covered.
- If anyone comes while you are absent, I'll cover for you.
- The government is clearly involved in a cover-up.

- Are you recovering from your sickness?
- I need to arrange breakdown cover.
- This must be done under cover of darkness.
- He was working as an under-cover agent.

Very often a cover-up is simply man's way of hiding himself and his sin when he feels wounded or guilty, but keeping matters in the dark does not bring peace or resolution of the issue. If you keep sweeping dirt under the carpet, the bumps eventually trip you up. However, when God covers, things are brought into the light so that truth, restoration and freedom can follow.

This book is not just an investigation of an interesting biblical concept. It is the result of a growing realization, as we have prayed with many people at Ellel Ministries centers, that an understanding of the principle of God's covering can be a wonderful key for the restoration of damaged lives. God wants to protect and nurture mankind and He has clearly revealed in His Word the way in which He can do this. Unfortunately, we have mostly chosen independence. The result has been a world of damaged lives, but God has put in place the most amazing plan to *re-cover* us.

The Bible describes this invisible shelter by painting written pictures. No one picture will fully describe the covering of God but each one provides an important perspective to give us a clearer understanding.

God's covering is a place of shade from a burning sun

In England, we tend to seek the sun rather than avoid it, especially when we are on our summer holidays. There have been many jokes about our English summers, which can often give us more of a soaking than a scorching! Things may of course be changing as we face global warming; maybe we will all soon be seeking to avoid the sun's heat.

In many parts of the world the burning sun can be relentless and destructive. People traveling through desert areas long for an opportunity to find rest in a place of shade. The sensation of moving from the intense but invisible radiation of the sun to the cool relief of some shade has been experienced by most of us at some time. The psalmist says that this is a good way to picture the protection which comes when God covers our lives from all that would damage us in this spiritually hostile world:

> *The LORD is your keeper;*
> *The LORD is your shade on your right hand.*
> *The sun will not smite you by day,*
> *Nor the moon by night.*

> (Psalm 121:5–6)

In Psalm 91 there are wonderful insights into the reality of God's covering. To set the scene the writer begins by telling us that the shelter which God provides, for those who dwell in covenant with Him, is the place of His shadow or the shade of His presence. What an awesome thought, that God's shadow can provide a world-wide protection from a spiritual radiation which will harm us.

> *He who dwells in the shelter of the Most High*
> *Will abide in the shadow of the Almighty.*

> (Psalm 91:1)

Isaiah similarly prophesies that God's people will experience His protection like a canopy over their lives:

> *There will be a shelter to give shade from the heat by day, and refuge and protection from the storm and the rain.*

> (Isaiah 4:6)

The idea of a refuge from a storm suggests another picture of His covering as being like a place to shelter in a torrential downpour. We will return to the theme of umbrellas later in this book!

God's covering is a cloak covering our nakedness

In an extraordinary picture of the unhappy history of the city and the people of Jerusalem, God describes, through Ezekiel, His deep desire to deal with the exposed condition of His people. He likens their story to the life of a young girl born into an uncaring family and left exposed. In due course, she is offered a covenant of protection by a loving husband:

> *"As for your birth, on the day you were born your navel cord was not cut, nor were you washed with water for cleansing; you were not rubbed with salt or even wrapped in cloths . . . Then I passed by you and saw you, and behold, you were at the time for love; so I spread My skirt over you and covered your nakedness. I also swore to you [gave you My solemn oath] and entered into a covenant with you so that you became Mine," declares the Lord GOD.*
>
> (Ezekiel 16:4, 8)

Sadly, the story goes on to describe the girl's rejection of this offer of covering, as she chooses other lovers. When a man falls in love with a young woman and looks towards marriage, he becomes jealous of any attention given to her by other suitors. He wants her hidden beauty to be for his eyes only. God frequently likens Himself to a husband of His people, longing to see the fulfillment of the deep relationship which He has always purposed for us. We also see here in this passage from Ezekiel an important connection between covering and covenant. God has expressed His love towards mankind by establishing a covenant with us which provides for our permanent well-being as we respond to Him.

The spiritual clothing which God has provided for us is not just to cover our nakedness but also to give us dignity and authority. His cloak over our lives is a mark of the significance and value which He places on us. Clothing has always been used as a means of declaring authority; a policeman is recognized, for example, by his uniform. Scripture refers to a mantle resting on those whom God has chosen for a purpose. This is seen nowhere more clearly than in the life of the prophet Elisha:

> *He [Elisha] also took up the mantle of Elijah that fell from him and returned and stood by the bank of the Jordan.*
>
> (2 Kings 2:13)

God wants the garment of His authority in our lives to be recognized by the powers and principalities of the heavenly realms.

God's covering even gives beauty to our lives. Many people go to extraordinary lengths to adorn their bodies in an attempt to be attractive to those around them. However, each of us will have met people who radiate a simple godly beauty, not because of their physical clothing but through the garment which comes from their relationship with Jesus. He wants the very best for His bride. The clothing Jesus provides for us cannot be bettered by our own efforts and we can delight in the garments He gives us, as the prophet Isaiah did:

> *I will rejoice greatly in the LORD,*
> *My soul will exult in my God;*
> *For He has clothed me with garments of salvation,*
> *He has wrapped me with a robe of righteousness,*
> *As a bridegroom decks himself with a garland,*
> *And as a bride adorns herself with her jewels.*
>
> (Isaiah 61:10)

God's covering is the wing of a mother hen

One day Jesus was moved to ponder the condition of the city of Jerusalem and her rebellious inhabitants. His heart was breaking at the desolation which was to come because God's instructions for her protection had been rejected and He cried out,

> *"Jerusalem, Jerusalem, who kills the prophets and stones those who are sent to her! How often I wanted to gather your children together,*

the way a hen gathers her chicks under her wings, and you were unwilling. Behold, your house is being left to you desolate."

(Matthew 23:37–38)

His words express such a deep longing to cover the people and shelter them from all that is against them, but God cannot cover those who choose to be independent from Him.

How extraordinary, but how appropriate, that God would liken Himself to a mother hen. My wife, Denise, and I lived in the highlands of Scotland for many years and we always kept chickens. Our children loved to see the chicks hatch out and begin to explore the world around the coop. However, that world included birds of prey, foxes, cats, rain and sometimes snow. To see the boldness of the mother hen, spreading out her feathers and wings to shield the returning chicks, was quite amazing. Whatever the conditions or the opposition, any attempt to dislodge her from this place of protection was met with determined resistance and a sharp peck at the intruder.

Interestingly, Psalm 91 uses the same analogy to declare God's character as protector, no matter what tactics the enemy might employ to entrap us:

For it is He who delivers you from the snare of the trapper
And from the deadly pestilence.
He will cover you with His pinions [feathers],
And under His wings you may seek refuge:
His faithfulness is a shield and bulwark.

(vv. 3–4)

How precious are these wonderful truths about our Maker and His faithfulness to bring His children back under His covering. Absolutely nothing can overwhelm our God. What a perfect place to find safety!

God's covering is a dwelling place in a storm

I can remember the incident so clearly. I was seventeen years old and walking with a group of friends in a remote area of the Western

Isles of Scotland. We had set up an overnight camp halfway up a mountain on a small patch of grass by a stream. Our tent was, we believed, designed to withstand storms, but we were careful to anchor the guy-lines with small boulders. As we lay in our sleeping bags we were able to hear, all too easily, the strengthening wind and the growing intensity of the rain. At around midnight, with no warning, a particularly strong gust of wind tore the guys from their fixings and we were left totally exposed to the fierce storm which had developed. It was very frightening as we (and all our belongings) were suddenly battered by the wind and rain.

How I longed, in that moment, to be scooped up and taken to a safe, solid dwelling with a sound roof. I realize now that God wants exactly that place of spiritual protection for each of us when we experience life's storms. Scripture assures us:

> *"There is none like the God of Jeshurun,*
> *Who rides the heavens to your help,*
> *And through the skies in His majesty.*
> *The eternal God is a dwelling place,*
> *And underneath are the everlasting arms . . . "*

(Deuteronomy 33:26–27)

For that group of us exposed on the Scottish mountains, God's help was not something we understood then. We could only do our best to recover the situation by our own effort, as we scrambled in the dark looking for our scattered possessions. After some time, we did find the tent and sufficient poles to give minimal protection for the rest of the night, but I never forgot the intensity of experiencing such sudden exposure when I had thought I was safe. Actually, I continued to carry within me an unconscious and unhealed fear and distress from that night. I was physically exposed to a storm all those years ago but I was still living with the spiritual exposure that had taken a hold of me and had left me in a place of disquiet.

I did not know Jesus then and I didn't seek His protection that night, but recently I had an opportunity to put the whole incident into the Lord's hands. For the first time I was able to know His covering and restoration over a part of me that had for so long carried the trauma of what had happened some forty years before. The night of the disappearing tent has now become a healed memory and I have found release from the fears and distress of this painful incident.

It is this kind of healing which we will be exploring. We will look at how we can experience restoration of God's covering for the incidents in our lives which have caused us both physical and spiritual exposure. We may not have realized the significance of what happened at the time, but spiritual issues are outside time and can be affecting us today, holding us trapped in the traumas of the past.

Interestingly, the apostle Paul speaks about tents and their temporary quality as he reflects on the transient nature of this mortal life:

> *For we know that if the earthly tent which is our house is torn down, we have a building from God, a house not made with hands, eternal in the heavens.*
>
> (2 Corinthians 5:1)

How wonderful! I don't need to be troubled any more by the uncertainty of tents, because God has given me a permanent dwelling to rest in.

Storms are frightening and damaging. Man is designed to need a safe home with a sound roof, both physically and spiritually. God wants us to be in a right place with Him and find peace in His provision of a secure dwelling. Through the prophet Isaiah He promises:

> *The fruit of righteousness will be peace;*
> *the effect of righteousness will be quietness and confidence*
> *forever.*
> *My people will live in peaceful dwelling places,*
> *in secure homes,*
> *in undisturbed places of rest.*

Though hail flattens the forest
and the city is leveled completely,
how blessed you will be . . .

(Isaiah 32:17–20 NIV)

Secure homes are wonderful but we need to look a little more closely at what these hailstorms represent. Outside God's covering the spiritual weather can be very hostile. What are these spiritual realms which have such a significant effect on our lives?

The hostile places in the spiritual realms

There is no neutral spiritual territory in the whole of God's creation. In Acts 26, Jesus explains to Paul that, through disobedience, human beings have separated themselves from the spiritual realm of light and peace under God's covering, and taken themselves into the hostile realm of darkness and disorder which is ruled by Satan. Paul is to be sent on a rescue mission, "to open their eyes so that they may turn from darkness to light and from the dominion of Satan to God" (Acts 26:18).

This realm of darkness is under the authority of Satan because he was handed a right to rule in this disobedient world, through the rebellion of man. When he was tempting Jesus in the wilderness, he said to Him,

"I will give You all this domain and its glory; for it has been handed over to me, and I give it to whomever I wish."

(Luke 4:6)

Jesus did not disagree with Satan's statement about his authority in this world, but He certainly did disagree with the offer of receiving this domain by giving Satan worship. Like many who are out to steal and destroy, the enemy fights under cover of darkness, the realm of the occult. Jesus has the victory by walking in the light!

God's plan for human beings was for them to be safe within the boundaries of divine covenant protection. He gave human beings the freedom to choose, but made clear to Adam how to stay right with God and to depend on God's wisdom: "but from the tree of the knowledge of good and evil you shall not eat, for in the day that you eat from it you will surely die" (Genesis 2:17). However, Adam, and his descendants, chose to break covenant with God and follow the instructions of Satan, prompting God to say through the prophet Hosea:

> *But like Adam they have transgressed the covenant;*
> *There they have dealt treacherously against Me.*
>
> (Hosea 6:7)

It is a foundational truth that we come under the authority of whoever we choose to obey. Obeying Satan's instruction to eat forbidden fruit radically changed the spiritual authority over the life of man. Mankind was separated from the life-giving spiritual covering of God and bound into a lifeless world of spiritual darkness. Jesus makes very clear who is the spiritual ruler of a world which chooses to remain in rebellion to God:

> *"I will not speak much more with you, for the ruler of the world is coming, and he has nothing in Me."*
>
> (John 14:30)

Most of mankind is blind to the enemy's rule in this world, but it remains nonetheless a fact of spiritual life which needs further exploring.

Summary

A desire for the right spiritual covering of mankind is at the very heart of God's plans and purposes. He likens Himself to a prospective husband, passionately desiring to protect the purity of his bride. Like an unfaithful lover, mankind has turned away from the covenant promises of God and, in so doing, has become exposed to the spiritual hostility of this fallen world with all the consequent damage.

To help us understand the significance of His covering and the effect of our being exposed, God has given written pictures in the Bible. These help us to be aware of the light and the dark, the good and the bad of the spiritual realms, which have such an important effect on our lives.

The Bible describes the special shelter of God in many ways, including a place of shade, the wing of a bird, clothing of dignity and a safe dwelling. He wants us to know that there truly is an answer to the cry of our hearts for a place of spiritual safety and healing. Before we explore His promises to cover us, we need to look at the reality of spiritual exposure.

CHAPTER 2

What is spiritual exposure?

Getting the whole picture

Understanding our enemy

The name Satan means "adversary of God." This describes a powerful spiritual being who chose to rebel against God's instructions. We can understand a little of this rebellion and the character of this spiritual being when we look at individuals on earth who have chosen profoundly rebellious lives.

Isaiah prophesies about the wickedness and the destiny of the king of Babylon. It becomes clear that there is a dark spiritual power behind the choices of this king, driving him to extremes of rebellion against God:

> *"How you have fallen from heaven,*
> *O star of the morning [Lucifer], son of the dawn!*
> *You have been cut down to the earth,*
> *You who have weakened the nations!*
> *But you said in your heart,*
> *'I will ascend to heaven;*
> *I will raise my throne above the stars of God,*
> *And I will sit on the mount of assembly*
> *In the recesses of the north.*

> *I will ascend above the heights of the clouds;*
> *I will make myself like the Most High.' "*
>
> (Isaiah 14:12–13)

What pride and arrogance are displayed here! How well the prophet describes the fall and character of Lucifer who desired to oppose and even usurp Almighty God!

Satan is a created spiritual being in gross rebellion against God, confined to operate in the realm of disobedience and darkness, a domain which is spiritually hostile to us. All things have been created by God; there is nothing that lies outside His creation. However, within this vast spiritual and physical creation there is this realm of darkness, separated from the covering and protective hand of God. This hostile realm, under the rule of Satan, is described in many different ways throughout Scripture.

We will have a look at some of the pictures the Bible uses to describe how man is exposed when he steps outside God's covering. In fact the physical world around us is not just useful in illustrating the truths of the spiritual realms, but we discover that the *seen realms* are actually a reflection of the *unseen realms*. What happens in the spiritual domain has an outworking in the physical world. For example, the fruitfulness or barrenness of people's lives, and indeed the land which they occupy, often reflects the spiritual condition of their hearts.

The Bible tells us that this is true. In Deuteronomy 28:1, 4 it says, for example,

> " . . . *if you diligently obey the* LORD *your God, being careful to do all His commandments, which I command you today . . . Blessed shall be the offspring of your body and the produce of your ground . . .* "

In the same way that we have been looking at biblical pictures to describe God's covering, we will now explore more pictures which describe exposure to Satan's realm.

Spiritual exposure is a storm battering our lives

God has created all things, even storms. He wants the very best for us, a place of safety in Him, but in our rebellion we find ourselves subject to some very hostile aspects of His creation. God has ordained that mankind has a choice to obey Him or disobey Him. If God permits disobedience, His creation must include the consequence of that disobedience, *that is,* spiritual and physical exposure. The effect of this distressing exposure may, or may not, be that man chooses to turn back to God, to find again the peace which He gives:

> *"I smote you and every work of your hands with blasting wind, mildew and hail; yet you did not come back to Me," declares the LORD.*
>
> (Haggai 2:17)

I remember some years ago visiting Sydney, Australia, a few weeks after an exceptional hailstorm had crossed part of the city. The dents in the cars gave clear evidence of the huge size of the hailstones. Thankfully it was property rather than people that suffered most damage, although many Christians saw the storm as displaying God's wrath regarding particular sinful activities within the city. This was a reasonable conclusion when we remember how often the Bible refers to hailstorms as God's instrument of wrath, the consequence of man's disobedience to His covenant. The prophet Isaiah writes, for example:

> *Behold, the Lord has a strong and mighty agent;*
> *As a storm of hail, a tempest of destruction,*
> *Like a storm of mighty overflowing waters,*
> *He has cast it down to the earth with His hand.*

Interestingly, the traditional corrugated metal roofs in Sydney faired rather better than the more modern tiling which shattered under the impact of the hail. God offers the safest type of roofing over our lives if we choose to stay right with Him. Pharaoh experienced the destructive power of hailstones as he resisted God's commands regarding the children of Israel. He also saw the extraordinary effect of God's covering hand over those who belonged to Him:

> _The hail struck all that was in the field through all the land of Egypt, both man and beast; the hail also struck every plant of the field and shattered every tree of the field. Only in the land of Goshen, where the sons of Israel were, there was no hail. Then Pharaoh sent for Moses and Aaron, and said to them, "I have sinned this time; the LORD is the righteous one, and I and my people are the wicked ones."_
>
> (Exodus 9:25–27)

In recent years communities around the world seem to be experiencing more flooding than ever before. It is often a devastating experience. The feeling of desperation can be similar when there is a sense of being overwhelmed in our hearts. As the psalmist recognizes, it can feel just like a flood:

> _"Had it not been the LORD who was on our side,"_
> _Let Israel now say . . ._
> _"Then the raging waters would have swept over our soul."_
>
> (Psalm 124:1, 5)

Storms and flooding do much damage. They are not the place of safety that God wants for us. He is on our side against this devastation if we walk with Him.

Spiritual exposure is confrontation with an enemy wielding weapons of war

> _"Behold, I Myself have created the smith who blows the fire_
> _of coals_
> _And brings out a weapon for its work;_
> _And I have created the destroyer to ruin."_
>
> (Isaiah 54:16)

Satan is a created, though fallen, spiritual being at enmity with God and all His creation. There is a perpetual war being fought in the heavenly realms and, outside God's covering, it is a very dangerous battlefield. Jesus wants us to understand that we really are up against an enemy, although he is powerless against our Savior's true authority. He told His disciples:

> *"Behold, I have given you authority to tread on serpents and scorpions, and over all the power of the enemy, and nothing will injure you."*

> (Luke 10:19)

Paul frequently reminds us of the hostile battleground of the enemy's domain and he encourages us to look for godly protection:

> *Put on the full armor of God, so that you will be able to stand firm against the schemes of the devil. For our struggle is not against flesh and blood but against the rulers, against the powers, against the world forces of this darkness, against the spiritual forces of wickedness in the heavenly places.*

> (Ephesians 6:11–12)

Most people in this world have no concept that they are in a spiritual battle. They wander through the battlefield oblivious of the mines and shells, stumbling into dangerous and damaging situations. Sometimes they even seem to "get away with it" as they wander past the bomb craters. The reality of any war is that, if you appease the enemy as this world does, you may well experience less obvious hostility. In reality, however, you remain subject to his control and to the destiny which he chooses. When we decide to follow Jesus, we inevitably move into positions on the battlefield which actively oppose Satan and his followers. The hostility which we experience may well intensify. In the book of Revelation the apostle John refers to Satan's anger against those who seek to remain faithful to God's commands:

> *So the dragon was enraged with the woman, and went off to make war with the rest of her children, who keep the commandments of God and hold to the testimony of Jesus.*

(12:17)

The great news is, of course, that Jesus, the commander of the Lord's army, has defeated this spiritual enemy. When we truly obey what the commander says, we stand in a place which is safe from all that the enemy might throw at us. In Colossians 2:15 Paul affirms,

> *When He had disarmed the rulers and authorities, He made a public display of them, having triumphed over them through Him.*

It is so important for God's people to take seriously the reality of the flaming arrows of the evil one and to realize that protection only comes when we are under right cover. It is not something which need make us fearful, because we truly have the opportunity to stay under cover in the One who is indestructible. Paul describes that cover as armor; in fact it is the protection of Jesus Himself:

> *Therefore, take up the full armor of God, so that you will be able to resist in the evil day, and having done everything, to stand firm.*
> (Ephesians 6:13)

Spiritual exposure is a deathly garment

David experienced very dangerous situations during his journey towards becoming king. The hostility which he faced was frequently overwhelming, leaving him feeling helpless and desolate. He had nowhere to go to escape his predicament: all he could do was to cry out to God:

> *I cry aloud with my voice to the LORD;*
> *I make supplication with my voice to the LORD.*

I pour out my complaint before Him;
I declare my trouble before Him.
When my spirit was overwhelmed within me,
You knew my path.
In the way where I walk
They have hidden a trap for me.

(Psalm 142:1–3)

The word "overwhelmed" which is used in this passage literally means "shrouded." The enemy's darkness can be like a smothering garment which seems to trap us and rob us of life. I remember obstacle races at school which included crawling under a long tarpaulin. As a little child it seemed a very frightening place, scrambling for light at the end of this clinging tunnel.

It is interesting that during the initiation ceremony of Freemasonry the candidate is instructed to remove his normal clothing and dress in humiliating garments. The ritual then requires him to accept a hood over his head, representing the darkness from which the "enlightenment" of Freemasonry is supposed to release him. In fact, permitting this hood to be placed over their eyes has taken many men into deep spiritual blindness. Different types of clothing can be a potent symbol of spiritual covering. When the garments (and therefore the spiritual cover) are not what God intended, the enemy is given rights to control a part of our lives. Satan's covering is always a place of bondage, defilement and deception.

We shall be exploring later in this book how some people experience a cloak of shame which robs them of abundant life. One such person was the psalmist who wrote:

My dishonor is continually before me,
And the shame of my face has covered me . . .

(Psalm 44:15 NKJV)

The enemy is not creative. He only distorts and perverts what God has created. God desires dignified robes for the covering of His children but the enemy seeks to constrain us in grave clothes.

Spiritual exposure is wearing wrong clothes or even no clothes

An obvious sin, which literally involves nakedness, is adultery. But the issue extends well beyond the exposing of ourselves physically. God frequently compares sexual sin with idolatry, as the following passage from Ezekiel chapter 16 illustrates:

> *Then the word of the LORD came to me, saying, "Son of man, make known to Jerusalem her abominations . . . Because your lewdness was poured out and your nakedness uncovered through your harlotries with your lovers and with all your detestable idols, and because of the blood of your sons which you gave to idols . . . "*
>
> (vv. 1, 2 and 36)

Both sexual sin and idolatry involve the surrender of our identity in ways which leave us very exposed, maybe physically, but certainly spiritually.

Similarly in the book of Lamentations, Jeremiah expresses God's distress at the spiritual desolation Jerusalem has brought upon herself:

> *Jerusalem sinned greatly,*
> *Therefore she has become an unclean thing.*
> *All who honored her despise her*
> *Because they have seen her nakedness;*
> *Even she herself groans and turns away.*
>
> (1:8)

Through the prophets, God is desperate to make His people understand the serious spiritual consequence of His people offering themselves to false gods. They are literally stepping out of the covenant protection which He has offered them, as surely as a wife breaking covenant with her husband through adultery. Such activity is painful for God and leaves His people dangerously exposed. It couldn't be expressed more clearly: sin, especially idolatry, leaves you spiritually naked.

The wrong clothes can leave us as exposed as if we had no clothes. Jesus tells a story of a marriage feast. Many who were invited refused to come, while others, just ordinary people, came to fill their places. Then comes a hard part of the story: one of the guests is seen to be improperly dressed and is unceremoniously thrown out:

> *"But when the king came in to look over the dinner guests, he saw a man there who was not dressed in wedding clothes . . . "*
>
> (Matthew 22:11)

Jesus is clearly telling the disciples that there is essential spiritual clothing for us if we truly desire to participate in His marriage feast with His bride.

I can imagine the man protesting that he had done his very best to smarten up for the festivities, but we need to remember that God was equally unimpressed with Adam's fig leaves. When God says that we need to be covered in a certain way, which only He can provide, we had better take note!

The good news is that we do not need to remain naked or wearing the wrong clothes; God has done all that is required to make available the very best robes. The question is: are we willing to put them on? It is amazing that the Creator of the universe has provided perfect clothing but most people still say, "I will choose my own wardrobe, thank You very much!"

God sees man's condition

Jesus has a strong message for the church at Laodicea: you think you've got everything covered in your life but actually you are walking around without the right spiritual clothes:

> *"Because you say, 'I am rich, and have become wealthy, and have need of nothing,' and you do not know that you are wretched and miserable and poor and blind and naked, I advise you to buy from Me gold refined by fire so that you may become rich, and white*

garments so that you may clothe yourself, and that the shame of your
nakedness will not be revealed . . . "

(Revelation 3:17–18)

We may see people dressed in fine garments which cover the body but God sees the spiritual covering over our hearts. Any good father wants his children to have the dignity of proper clothing. Physical and spiritual nakedness brings indignity and shame. God says that this is not right for His children. Isaiah had a remarkable gifting to speak out words which were from the very heart of God. So much pointless religious practice was being carried on by God's people that Isaiah found himself expressing the frustration of God as He longed for the people to see, and to deal with, the *real* needs among the people.

God was fed up with the show of ritual fasting:

"Is this not the fast which I choose,
To loosen the bonds of wickedness,
To undo the bands of the yoke,
And to let the oppressed go free
And break every yoke?
Is it not to divide your bread with the hungry
And bring the homeless poor into the house;
When you see the naked, to cover him;
And not to hide yourself from your own flesh?

(Isaiah 58:6–7)

Of course there would have been those with nothing to cover their physical bodies, but God was declaring that the nakedness among them was far more than just the absence of garments.

In Luke chapter 15, when the prodigal son returned home after losing everything, it was the need to cover him with the best robe that was top priority for the father. He hated to see the exposure, distress and embarrassment of his son. God feels the same about us.

What has all this got to do with me?

This principle of God's covering may be an interesting topic but how does it affect each one of us? As you read through this book you might like to ask yourself these questions:

- What has been the covering in my life?
- Were there times when the spiritual covering over my life was very different from what God intended?
- How did that affect me?
- How does God bring restoration of His covering into my life today?

Let me tell a true story here of a man we will call Tom. This is an example of how the principle of God's covering, or the lack of it, can seriously affect people's lives.

Tom was a pastor in his fifties and he came seeking prayer for an aggressive side to his character which occasionally, but dramatically, rose to the surface and deeply affected relationships with his family and those in his church. As we prayed with him, God began to reveal to Tom that he was carrying deep wounding from the relationship with his father, who had been unwilling to stand up for him at a critical time in his early childhood.

He was reminded of the day, at ten years old, when he was being bullied at school. When he got home he told his dad, expecting help, but, on this occasion, Tom's dad seemed not to take it seriously and told him that he would just have to learn to look after himself. As Tom remembered the incident he began to sob and kept repeating, "Dad, why didn't you come and fight for me?" It was a moment in his life when he desperately needed the godly protection of a dad, not necessarily to fight for him physically, but at least to stand up for him, in fact to cover him in a moment of vulnerability.

Tom went on to say he realized now that in the absence of Dad's godly covering, he had made an unconscious decision to fight for himself. In fact he had decided he would be his own protection.

Through Dad's sin of leaving him uncovered and unprotected, Tom chose a solution which was not God's way. Tom realized that he had spent his whole life, up to that moment of the prayer time, living by an inner vow that he would never allow himself to be in a place of vulnerability or weakness in *any* relationship.

As we continued to pray, Tom said something that was life-changing for him: "God, I want You to fight for me from now on, I give up doing it in my own strength." In terms of what we are looking at in this book, Tom was in effect saying, "God, You cover me, even in that painful place where I felt let down by my own father. Today I stop trying to cover myself and let You take over." Tom spoke out forgiveness of his father and he experienced a powerful encounter with the Lord as he received deliverance from the aggressive spiritual hold to which he had yielded all those years before. There was, from that day, a radical change in his character and a new place of peace in his heart.

The sense of exposure Tom felt as a child had caused him to decide subconsciously to be his own protector, even from an early age. In vowing to fight for himself he had chosen independence from the uncertain covering of his father, but this was not God's order for family life. Dad was at fault, but the sin of parents often causes their children to stumble. Praise God that there is healing for each one of us today! Later in this book we will be exploring more of this.

Summary

There is a spiritual realm ruled by Satan which is hostile to our well-being. We can picture it as a burning sun, a battering storm, an overwhelming flood, grave clothes or even no clothes at all. The truth is that there is an enemy who is in disobedience to God and to whom we are very vulnerable when we are out of God's covering.

God seeks to re-cover the lives of those who respond to Him. Every part of our being can be restored to the place of His protection and healing as we recognize the reasons why we became exposed and also understand what steps we need to take to receive His perfect shelter.

Let's look at the start of spiritual nakedness in human beings and then how it progressed in their lives.

How spiritual exposure started

We thought we knew best

Satan's beginnings

As we will see in a moment, Satan knows about covering and he certainly understands the significance of spiritual authority. Of course he has decided to rebel against God's commands and has eternally lost the position of authority which God had delegated to him. In Revelation 12:7–8 we are told:

> And there was war in heaven, Michael and his angels waging war with the dragon. The dragon and his angels waged war, and they were not strong enough, and there was no longer a place found for them in heaven.

What was Satan's position in heaven before his rebellion? Bible commentators see Isaiah chapter 14 and Ezekiel chapter 28 as giving very interesting clues. Both chapters are prophecies about the judgment upon earthly kings, but in these passages it becomes evident that the prophecy is describing the grossly evil character of the spiritual power that is working in and through these kings as they give over their lives to pride and arrogance.

We are being given a special insight into the relationship between God and this created spiritual being who takes the name Satan, the adversary of God. We looked previously at the Isaiah reference which described a little of the journey of this powerful spiritual being from having the name Lucifer to earning the name Satan. He was created to be a carrier of light, but as he sought to elevate himself, he lost the position which God had entrusted to him and became His enemy.

A very similar insight is given by Ezekiel:

> *"You were the anointed cherub who covers,*
> *And I placed you there.*
> *You were on the holy mountain of God;*
> *You walked in the midst of the stones of fire.*
> *You were blameless in your ways*
> *From the day you were created*
> *Until unrighteousness was found in you . . .*
> *Your heart was lifted up because of your beauty;*
> *You corrupted your wisdom by reason of your splendor.*
> *I cast you to the ground . . . "*
>
> (Ezekiel 28:14–16, 17)

How amazing that Satan himself once had a special place of authority to be a means of God's covering, in His very presence. Yet he chose to take pride in his position and his appearance and be independent of his Maker. Satan understands the importance of God's covering and he seeks to encourage man to join him in his independence. He still targets followers of Jesus and that includes you and me!

Man's beginnings

As the wonderful creation of humans occurs, God breathes life-giving spirit into physical matter and forms a living soul:

> *Then the LORD God formed man of dust from the ground, and breathed*
> *into his nostrils the breath of life; and man became a living being.*
>
> (Genesis 2:7)

He creates them male and female, not just to be observed by their Maker, but human beings made in the image of God for an intimate covenant relationship with Him.

God blessed them; He instructed them on their destiny; He delegated to them authority over the created earth; He gave plants for food; He gave understanding of cultivation; He gave boundaries for their safety; and He declared His deep satisfaction in this masterpiece of His creativity.

Babies come into the world naked but completely unperturbed by their nakedness because of their utter dependence on the protecting arms of their mother and father. Adam and Eve were similarly naked but initially they were so fully wrapped up in God's love that having no clothes did not matter to them:

> *And the man and his wife were both naked and were not ashamed.*
> (Genesis 2:25)

Now we must consider another amazing gift which God gave to man and woman. They were given free-will to choose either to receive all this wonderful protection and provision from their Creator, or to go independent. God desired above all that they would choose to dwell with Him and receive the life He was offering, but you can't have real relationship with someone by forcing them. God gave very clear instructions for their well-being but He also gave them the freedom to say *no*.

God's most important instruction was that they should depend totally on His knowledge of what was right or wrong for them. If they sought to depend on their own wisdom by eating from the tree of the knowledge of good and evil, then they would be rejecting His spiritual shelter and nurture which was sustaining their lives. They would still have a heavenly Father who loved them but, spiritually, they would be putting themselves outside the intimate protection of His household. With some encouragement from Satan, who saw an opportunity to usurp the authority given to man, they chose independence and found themselves immediately aware of their severe exposure and very afraid of the consequence:

> *He [man] said, "I heard the sound of You in the garden, and I was*
> *afraid because I was naked; so I hid myself."*

> (Genesis 3:10)

By taking the advice of Satan to eat the fruit God had forbidden, Adam and Eve joined Satan's independence movement and put themselves out of God's covering and under the spiritual authority of this fallen angel. What a huge mistake and what a consequence it had for them and all their descendants. Several times in the Gospel of John, Jesus calls Satan "the ruler of this world." It was man who handed him that title, giving away the authority to take charge of the created world – an authority which God had previously given to man.

Adam broke covenant with God and we all reaped the consequence

When man chose independence from God, his exposure became very evident and very painful. Adam and Eve were afraid because they were naked; they had stepped away from the spiritual covering which provided the nurture that God had prepared for them. The close relationship which God desires with man is described throughout the Bible as covenant. It is an expression of God's love for us and is a permanent commitment by Him to protect and provide for those whom He has created. It is God's way of declaring that He can, and will, provide all the cover we need for our well-being, but it remains our choice to accept it or reject it. We shall find out more about biblical covenant later in this book. Covenant and covering are inseparable aspects of God's relationship with mankind.

Adam and Eve did not just break away from the relationship which God had intended for them, they also broke covenant. Through the prophet Hosea God said,

> *But like Adam, they have transgressed the covenant;*
> *There they have dealt treacherously against Me.*

> (Hosea 6:7)

The breaking of any covenant has a spiritual consequence and the damage goes very deep. In the book of another prophet, Malachi, we read:

> *"Yet you say, 'For what reason?' Because the Lord has been a witness between you and the wife of your youth, against whom you have dealt treacherously, though she is your companion and your wife by covenant . . . Take heed then to your spirit, and let no one deal treacherously against the wife of your youth."*

> (2:14–15)

When a covenant is broken, the loss to our well-being can be very distressing and so it was for Adam and Eve. We are told that the sudden sense of exposure caused them to be afraid, something they had never felt before.

The fear which Adam and Eve experienced in their rebellion, is a God-given emotion which He provided for mankind so that we would know when we have stepped out of His covering. God has our well-being at the center of His purposes. So it was important to Him that, if we made wrong choices, we would be motivated to look for a place of safety, back in the arms of our Maker. But even here we have a choice. We may be motivated to look for a place of protection, but we can still choose to be self-sufficient. We may try fig leaves to deal with the embarrassment or we may look for our own place to hide, hoping to overcome the fears. The trouble is that outside God's covering we have not stepped into neutral spiritual territory, but into enemy territory.

It is only by following God's instructions that we put ourselves under His shelter. Whenever we are in disobedience, we are outside His covering. And outside His covering there exists a spiritual realm ruled by Satan. This right to rule was given to Satan through the disobedience of man. When Adam and Eve chose independence from God they were following Satan's instructions and giving over to him the very spiritual authority over this world which God had delegated to them. The world that is without Jesus now lives in the consequence of that decision, as Paul explains in Ephesians 2:1–2:

And you were dead in your trespasses and sins, in which you formerly walked according to the course of this world, according to the prince of the power of the air, of the spirit that is now working in the sons of disobedience.

Jesus often refers to this spiritual realm, ruled by Satan, as darkness. In fact we have noted before that the enemy only operates under cover of darkness, like many other thieves. Without light, deception is easy. Without light, we can apparently get away with wrongdoing without being seen. Without light, we can't see what is wounded or what is unclean. The darkness can seem very appealing when we have something to hide, but deep within ourselves we know somehow that it is not good to be without light.

It feels unsafe when you are in the dark

During the years my wife Denise and I lived in a remote farmhouse in the Highlands of Scotland my last task each day was to take our black Labrador for a short walk. We lived far from any street lights and some nights it was so dark that I could barely see anything ahead of me as I tentatively felt my way out of the gate and along the road to a small bridge over a stream which marked the furthest point of the walk.

I could occasionally hear the dog but never see him! On cold, sleeting winter nights the walk was uncomfortable and I couldn't wait to be back to a place of warmth and comfort. On the way towards the bridge there was very little to guide me and I would stumble on and off the road until I eventually knew from the sound of the rushing mountain stream that it was time to turn back.

Turning round was a significant moment. I could see the lights of the house. I had clear direction and the nearer that I got to the house the more comfortable I felt. How inviting was the protection of a warm, well-lit house. Our dog, Ben, nearly always got there first; I think he felt the same!

There was of course no great danger on these walks, but it is interesting how very important light is when you are walking in complete darkness. Thinking of those evening strolls gives me a simple picture of the spiritual exposure and darkness in which we travel when outside the home that God provides. In the dark I was quite oblivious to any unseen obstacles.

The warning signs

If part of our lives is in spiritual darkness and exposed just like Adam and Eve, there will probably be shame, anxiety or fear. In fact, until these are resolved, they can lie in a buried place within us, sometimes affecting the way we think and behave. These feelings are God's ways of drawing our attention to the need to look for a restoring of His cover. We shall look at these issues in more detail later but let's take a moment to consider the emotion of fear which warns us that we need a place of security. Love and fear cannot occupy the same location.

> *There is no fear in love; but perfect love casts out fear . . .*
> (1 John 4:18)

The moment that Adam and Eve were exposed by their disobedience, and separated from God's love, they felt fear.

If we let the place of fear motivate us into seeking God's covering, the fear is not needed any more and God's love can fill the place. I remember walking into a church some years ago on a sightseeing trip. It was full of idolatrous pictures and statues. I felt very uneasy and the person with me said, "What's your problem?" It was a feeling which can only be described as a troubling deep on the inside which warns you of danger.

In our family we used to call the feeling "butterflies" in the tummy. Jesus felt something similar as He sensed the presence of Satan prowling around, ready to use Judas to betray Him.

> *When Jesus had said this, He became troubled in spirit, and testified and said, "Truly, truly, I say to you, that one of you will betray Me."*
> (John 13:21)

As I looked around in that particular church, I knew that I was in spiritually hostile territory and that God wanted me to get outside. Sightseeing in this particular location, where Jesus was clearly not the focus of worship, was out of God's cover. Returning outside the church building, I was immediately at peace again.

Of course I could have ignored the feelings and pushed them aside by saying to myself that I did not need to be affected by such things. I could have told the friend with me that I was fine, covering up the feelings which I was experiencing. The problem is that when we ignore God and try to cover up the truth of what is happening to us, we bury the issue rather than resolve it. Adam discovered the same as he tried his own cover-up after finding himself exposed in the Garden of Eden:

> *Then the eyes of both of them were opened, and they knew that they were naked; and they sewed fig leaves together and made themselves loin coverings. They heard the sound of the LORD God walking in the garden in the cool of the day, and the man and his wife hid themselves from the presence of the LORD God among the trees of the garden.*
>
> (Genesis 3:7–8)

When God approached Adam and Eve, they felt no peace in the covering of their own leafy garments, so they still had a need to hide.

Fig leaves are worse than useless

Adam's fig leaves did not work. In fact fig leaves allow the problem to be concealed yet remain unresolved. This is a powerful picture of how we have all tried to deal with uncomfortable situations in our lives. Through ignorance, shame or pride, most of us have tried fig leaves (or the equivalent) to make ourselves feel better. Putting on *a brave face* may have seemed right at the time, but we were actually expressing unreality and that's just a form of cover up. Sins and wounds make us feel uncomfortable and we look for ways to conceal the guilt or the pain, especially when those around us may not be tolerant of our weaknesses. The truth is that we have sewn and worn fig leaves many times in our lives and thought it was the only solution.

For Adam and Eve, it was not until God provided skins by the sacrifice of an animal's life that they were able to be adequately clothed:

> *The* LORD *God made garments of skin for Adam and his wife, and clothed them.*
>
> (Genesis 3:21)

It is this profound truth which we can appropriate today in order to be "fully clothed" again, and at peace, in the places where our lives have been exposed by our wounds, our sin or the sins of others. God has provided the perfect sacrifice and covering, in Jesus, available to give a place of security to all who respond to His covenant offer. There is a very effective alternative to fig leaves if we care to receive God's solution.

Right clothing affirms identity

We have previously noted that there can be a significant connection between actual clothing and spiritual covering. The physical story of Adam and Eve, and how they were clothed, mirrored the spiritual condition of their existence. It is a fact that lives can become exposed by careless attention to clothing. One of the best examples of this in the Bible is the story of Joseph:

> *Now Israel loved Joseph more than all his sons, because he was the son of his old age; and he made him a varicolored tunic. His brothers saw that their father loved him more than all his brothers; and so they hated him and could not speak to him on friendly terms.*
>
> (Genesis 37:3–4)

Jacob expressed his favoritism towards Joseph by means of special clothing, but this was an ungodly attitude and an ungodly decision.

The special coat was a daily statement to the other brothers that they were of less value to Jacob. Far from giving Joseph valuable clothing, Jacob's actions simply exposed him to hostility through the inevitable jealousy of the rest of the family. There is a right way for parents to nurture their children which gives them a godly covering. When there is a distorted relationship, the consequences can be very damaging.

Of course, wrong relationships between parents and children need not necessarily involve clothing but sometimes it is exactly this issue which has been the focus of the dysfunctional attitudes. At Ellel Ministries centers, it is not unusual for us to find ourselves praying for men and woman who have been damaged in their sexual identity by being dressed inappropriately in the early years of their lives, often because the parents wanted a child of the opposite sex. Dressing a little boy as a girl not only provides wrong physical clothing but the sexual identity of the child is being left exposed to the hostile realm of the enemy. The behavior of parents towards their children, in every aspect of the relationship, is the means by which those children are either rightfully covered or left spiritually exposed. Clothing is not the only issue but it can sometimes be very significant, especially as it is meant to affirm both identity and dignity.

Leaving home in rebellion

Starting with the rebellion of Adam and Eve, the story of man, uncovered through disobedience, continues throughout the Bible. God found Israel's unfaithfulness very distressing. He provided all that she needed, including physical and spiritual food and clothing, but despite this Israel looked to false gods for the meeting of these needs. In Hosea 2:8–9 God laments:

> *"For she does not know that it was I who gave her the grain,*
> *the new wine and the oil,*
> *And lavished on her silver and gold,*
> *Which they used for Baal.*
> *Therefore, I will take back My grain at harvest time*

And My new wine in its season.
I will also take away My wool and My flax
Given to cover her nakedness."

Israel's unfaithfulness to God left her exposed in ways which she constantly failed to understand.

Jesus sums up the whole problem, and indeed the whole solution, in His amazing parable of the prodigal son in Luke chapter 15. It is a picture of God's children, given opportunity for relationship with the Father, making the choice of rebellion and independence, experiencing the despair of nakedness and finally responding to God's offer of recovery and restoration. Incidentally the older son in this story discovers that it is possible to miss the father's love without even leaving home!

This classic story from the Bible graphically describes the consequence of the younger son's rebellious heart which seeks independence from the rightful place of protection in a godly family. Money does not provide a secure alternative and the son finds himself increasingly vulnerable to the hostility of a world which opposes God's order and covering. He loses everything, not least his dignity. Then he reflects for a moment on the protection and provision available to everyone in his father's household. How would he be received if he went home? Admitting his rebellion, he begins a walk of faith.

"But when he came to his senses, he said, 'How many of my father's hired men have more than enough bread, but I am dying here with hunger! I will get up and go to my father, and will say to him, "Father, I have sinned against heaven, and in your sight; I am no longer worthy to be called your son; make me as one of your hired men."'"

(Luke 15:17–19)

The son returned to his father's home exposed and very vulnerable to the accusations of neighbors and indeed of his older brother. As a rebellious son, his actions warranted his being stoned to death, according to the law. The father, who has been watching and waiting for the home-coming, eagerly covers this exposure by receiving his dirty son and by declaring immediate personal protection. He gives his son his best cloak to hide the place of guilt and shame. The special robe which was placed around him, together with the ring and the sandals, restored the son's place in the family. This exactly speaks of the Father's heart for each one of us.

Our Father God sees every place of spiritual nakedness in the lives of His children. What do I mean by spiritual nakedness? Even as Christians, we can be carrying places of spiritual exposure and damage, as a consequence of the sinfulness of the world in which we have lived. Sometimes we have tried to apply our own covering but this can actually just leave us blind to the real need for God's intervention, until, like the prodigal son, we *come to our senses*.

The principles of spiritual covering apply to real lives today

When the first man and woman disobeyed God's instructions they felt exposed and fearful. They were not the last ones to have this experience. Whenever we disobey God's commands, or we are injured by someone else doing so, we feel uncomfortable. This feeling of exposure doesn't go away. Of course we have all tried to belittle the problem and get on with life, but the issues remain unresolved until Jesus is invited to restore the situation.

Let me give an example of how unresolved exposure in the past can affect our lives today. A man, whom I will call Ben, asked for help with a problem which he had concerning his lack of confidence in his masculinity. For no apparent reason, even at the age of fifty, he felt somehow ashamed of his own body.

We decided to pray together. He then remembered an incident which was a bit embarrassing for him to share. At the age of ten, he had been traveling home on a train with an older boy who had dared Ben to drop his trousers and show his genitals. Ben felt very intimidated and foolish. He knew that his parents would not want him to do this, but when the older boy offered a little money, it was too much for him and he did what was asked. The older boy, enjoying his control of the situation, laughed and ridiculed Ben, who went home very troubled by what had happened. He buried the memory because it was too embarrassing to think about. Occasionally, he had remembered the incident and felt again something of the intimidation of the older boy. It was as if, spiritually, a part of his life was trapped in the exposure of that day.

Why had God reminded Ben of this moment which had occurred so long before? We felt sure that it was God's time to re-cover Ben from the spiritual exposure and the distress which had stayed with him all those years. As we prayed, Ben forgave the older boy, confessed his own disobedience towards his parents and (hardest of all) he forgave himself for being weak and willing to be exposed for the gaining of a few pennies.

We asked Jesus to break the unresolved spiritual control of the older boy and to cover again that vulnerable moment of Ben's life and to restore his dignity, confidence and self-worth. It was a precious moment for Ben as he experienced release from the intimidation and felt the fear and shame leave. He could at last be fully at peace with the body which God had given him. Ben commented sometime later how significant had been the change which God had brought about through the prayer time.

As it happens, this story involved actual exposure of the physical body, but spiritual exposure can happen for many different reasons as we step out from God's covering or find ourselves unprotected. We shall explore more of this in a later chapter as we consider how this whole subject might have affected us personally.

Summary

The spiritual exposure of man started in the Garden of Eden. When Adam and Eve broke God's commands they also broke covenant with Him (a covenant which had provided them with protection). The initial consequence of this was for them to feel fear and shame. God intended that these feelings would motivate mankind to look for His covering again and be restored into the covenant relationship.

Throughout the Bible, however, God's people mostly chose independence and made the decision to provide the covering for themselves, just as Adam did with the fig leaves. But they all found that it did not bring peace, as it is only God who has got the perfect solution for man's exposure.

Clothes are important. They give a sense of identity and dignity. Although not the only issue through which we can become spiritually exposed, inappropriate physical clothing does affect our well-being. Whatever our past experiences, even Christians can be carrying the consequence of times in their lives when they have felt exposed. God's heart is to re-clothe us spiritually in those places so that we can walk on, with His peace and His confidence.

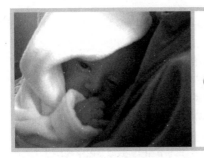

CHAPTER 4

God's response to man's exposure

Covenant and covering

God hated to see His children spiritually exposed

In the story of the prodigal son, the father couldn't wait to place the best robe around the exposed body of his precious son. From the moment that man lost his spiritual covering in the Garden of Eden, God embarked on an amazing recovery program to bring His children into the knowledge and experience of His covenant and His covering. The journey would be profound and very costly. There was going to be a lot for man to understand, but he continued to have the choice to listen and follow God's ways, or to follow the ways of the world. Let's trace that story through the Bible and see how important these principles are to God.

Adam and Eve learned that covering was costly

There is no quick fix to the absence of God's covering, lost when we rebel against His commands. Romans 6:23 tells us that *the wages of sin is death*. It is a serious issue, a matter of life and death. God's relationship with Adam and Eve was to be an intimate and life-giving covenant. There is nothing casual about covenant and God made very clear the terms of this agreement, how mankind could wonderfully benefit from God's day-by-day protection and provision.

However, Adam and Eve chose to do it their way, as men and women did many times after that.

We have noted that, in order to bring God's justice in response to sin, yet restore relationship with His creation, blood needed to be shed. God's people would later come to understand the significance of this much more. For the time being God made it clear that the fig leaves had to go and His provision of animal skins was the only right clothing. Expelled from Eden and separated from the intimacy of God's presence, man walked in a tenuous relationship with his Maker, progressively exploring wickedness and violence. Eventually God's grief brought Him to a dramatic decision to flood the earth and to destroy mankind, together with all the corruption.

Noah learned that God's covering was life-saving

As God viewed this corrupt world, one man, Noah, found favor in the eyes of the Lord. He was given detailed instructions by God for the protection of his family from the massive destruction that was coming on the earth. Noah discovered a simple truth: if you follow God's commands, you find the blessing of His protection. In this case the specific protection which the whole family (including the animal cargo) most needed, was a waterproof vessel to withstand the worldwide flood.

In addition to guidance about the timber construction of an ark, God gave one very special instruction. Noah was commanded to cover the vessel with a waterproofing agent:

> *"Make for yourself an ark of gopher wood; you shall make the ark with rooms, and shall cover it inside and out with pitch."*
>
> (Genesis 6:14)

In fact the Hebrew word used for this covering appears many times again in the story of God's people. *Kaphar*, meaning "to cover" (specifically here with pitch or bitumen), is the same word that is translated in other parts of the Bible as "to make atonement."

What a clear picture this is of the physical and spiritual barrier that Noah and his family needed to withstand the destruction which was coming on mankind. The simple reason given for Noah and his family being uniquely saved from the flood was that he walked with God:

> *Noah was a righteous man, blameless in his time; Noah walked with God.*
>
> (Genesis 6:9)

In other words, because Noah sought to keep right with God, he experienced divine covering over the whole family. Noah himself was not the covering, but his obedience to God's commands secured the shelter which they needed. This is a powerful principle: when there is godly order in a family and when the head of a household is right with the Lord, the whole family benefits from God's protection.

In fact God declared that His command to build a boat, and Noah's obedience, were the basis of a renewed covenant relationship which God wanted with this remnant of the human race:

> *"I will establish My covenant with you; and you shall enter the ark – you and your sons and your wife, and your sons' wives with you."*
>
> (Genesis 6:18)

It is interesting that God emphasized the need to *enter* the ark. God will always provide a place of shelter for His children but they *do* have to choose to enter that place of protection. Noah *did* follow God and *did* follow His commands, so his family *were* kept safe. God even declared, with the sign of a rainbow, that this covenant of protection from the same devastation would be enjoyed by all Noah's descendants. Here is another powerful principle: when we follow God's commands, the blessing of His covenant and His covering extends to the generations which come from us.

> *Then God spoke to Noah and to his sons with him, saying, "Now behold, I Myself do establish My covenant with you, and with your descendants after you . . .*
>
> (Genesis 9:8–9)

There is a remarkable similarity between the saving of Noah's family from drowning in the flood and the later protection of the child Moses, from drowning in the River Nile. In both cases God knew of the impending destruction and established His plan of protection, to *cover* a floating vessel with pitch, not only to save lives but to change the course of history. When God instructs us as to how we should establish His protective covering, it is really worth listening!

However, Noah's descendants were soon challenging God's authority, in the story of the tower of Babel (Genesis 11:1–9). It is amazing how important man feels when he builds a tall tower. Even today nations compete with one another to display their superiority by constructing the highest building on the planet. High places have always given the enemy an opportunity to display his pride. God was not impressed with the tower of Babel or man's desire for a universal language. God needed to show mankind how He alone would give man significance and safety. He planned to establish a covenant people and through them display His love, His protection and His provision.

Abraham learned that God's covering comes through covenant

God gave fresh revelation about the significance of covenant when He spoke to a man called Abram, changed his name to Abraham and said that He wanted to enter into a special agreement with him and his descendants. This was not just a relationship in which God would protect His children from a particular disaster but a promise to restore permanent intimacy between man and God.

It would of course eventually be completed through Jesus, but God chose Abraham to establish this promise. It was to bring about a remarkable inheritance for God's people, including possession of land. Abraham was not sure that he could trust God, until God began the process of making a covenant:

> *He [Abraham] said, "O Lord GOD, how may I know that I will possess it?" So He [God] said to him, "Bring Me a three year old heifer . . .*
> (Genesis 15:8–9)

Covenant in biblical times was serious. It went far beyond normal contracts and friendships. Covenant was a permanent, life-and-death matter. As God passed between the parts of a ritual sacrifice (a significant aspect for declaring covenant) Abraham knew that God meant business.

The foundational commitment of God in this covenant was that He would reveal Himself to *be God* to Abraham and to his descendants, on the understanding that they would follow His commands. In particular He would provide land, to be a place of safety and provision for this covenant people:

> *"I will establish My covenant between Me and you and your descendants after you throughout their generations for an everlasting covenant, to be God to you and to your descendants after you. I will give to you and your descendants after you, the land of your sojournings, all the land of Canaan, for an everlasting possession; and I will be their God."*
> (Genesis 17:7–8)

In a passage which we noted earlier, Ezekiel summarizes this relationship using an intimate picture of a young woman born into an environment of neglect and exposure, needing the strong protection of a marriage covenant. Let's remind ourselves again how clearly this passage links covenant and covering:

> *"As for your birth, on the day you were born your navel cord was not cut, nor were you washed with water for cleansing; you were not rubbed with salt or even wrapped in cloths . . . I made you numerous like plants of the field. Then you grew up, became tall . . . Yet you*

were naked and bare. Then I passed by you and saw you, and behold,
you were at the time for love; so I spread My skirt over you and covered
your nakedness. I also swore to you and entered into a covenant
*with you so that you became Mine," declares the Lord G*OD*. "Then I*
bathed you with water, washed off your blood from you and anointed
you with oil."

(Ezekiel 16:4, 7–9)

Here is another precious principle: when God covers and His covenant is established with His people, there is opportunity for anointing and cleansing. We can confidently say that God's covering is a place for His healing.

God's people learned that only God's covering brings true deliverance

By the time we come to the book of Exodus, God's covenant people have become slaves in Egypt, but God has a plan for deliverance. This involves drastic measures to safeguard His people and also to illustrate to them the cost of God's protective covering over their lives. The plan was called the Lord's Passover.

"The blood shall be a sign for you on the houses where you live; and
when I see the blood I will pass over you, and no plague will befall
you to destroy you when I strike the land of Egypt."

(Exodus 12:13)

We see again in this story an inescapable principle, as God chooses to re-cover and protect His people. To deal with the judgment of death, which is a consequence of sin, there has to be a sacrifice, the taking of a life. The instructions of God to the children of Israel required blood from a sacrificed animal to be put around the doorway of their houses.

Only the use of blood would protect them from plague and destruction. God's covering is very costly for the one that is sacrificed. We now understand that it was to be Jesus who would eventually be the perfect sacrifice and the provider of the blood, which would meet the justice of God. Jesus has now brought God's final solution for the recovering of man from the spiritual death that hangs over this rebellious world. When we are hidden in Christ Jesus, the perfect blood sacrifice, we discover the ultimate place of God's forgiveness, covering and healing.

God's people learned about exposure in the desert – for a long time

Following the Passover, God takes the children of Israel out of slavery, through the leadership of Moses, and He renews covenant with them:

> *"Now then, if you will indeed obey My voice and keep My covenant, then you shall be My own possession among all the peoples, for all the earth is Mine . . .*

> (Exodus 19:5)

Unfortunately, when the spies bring back reports of the giants in the Promised Land, the people fear them more than they fear God. Because of this disobedience, the exposure of the desert had to be endured for a further forty years. None of them, except Caleb and Joshua, would enter into the destiny that God had prepared for them.

God did not abandon His covenant with them or His protection over them, but most of them missed the best that He had prepared for them. He had offered a permanent place of safety and provision, but they would only experience God's temporary shelter. In the hardship of the desert God still demonstrated His covering through a portable tabernacle. He was their protection in the covering of a cloud during the day and a fire at night. This was the *shekinah* of God.

> *Now on the day that the tabernacle was erected the cloud covered the tabernacle, the tent of the testimony, and in the evening it was like the appearance of fire over the tabernacle, until morning.*

> (Numbers 9:15)

God's covering is a consequence of being in covenant with Him. Covenant is dependent on the participants keeping the terms of the agreement. God never breaks a promise and He gave His people clear commands as to how they could keep right with Him. Moses received the instructions and passed them on to the people:

> *"So He declared to you His covenant which He commanded you to perform, that is, the Ten Commandments; and He wrote them on two tablets of stone. The Lord commanded me at that time to teach you statutes and judgments, that you might perform them in the land where you are going over to possess it."*
>
> (Deuteronomy 4:13–14)

Unfortunately, from that time onwards God's people were more consistent in breaking the commands than keeping them.

The people learned that God's covering is a consequence of obedience

God continued to explain His foundational spiritual laws to His people, this covenant people. These were unchangeable spiritual laws such as the consequence of idolatry in the family line:

> *". . . for I, the LORD your God, am a jealous God, visiting the iniquity of the fathers on the children, on the third and the fourth generations of those who hate Me, but showing lovingkindness to thousands, to those who love Me and keep My commandments."*
>
> (Exodus 20:5b–6)

God gave them clear instructions about how to make sure things would go right for them by respecting these laws.

> *"You shall not make for yourself an idol, or any likeness of what is in heaven above or on the earth beneath or in the water under the earth."*
>
> (Exodus 20:4)

God's commands are like warning notices at the edge of a steep cliff, telling walkers to go no further. If they choose to disobey the warning signs, they will soon discover a distressing aspect to the law of gravity! God has established spiritual and physical laws which are intended to bless us. Gravity is an amazing physical law, literally holding everything together, but if we don't respect this law, it can be fatal. God's law of generational blessing is a wonderful promise of a godly inheritance, but we are told that the same law can bring iniquity into the family line, when there has been idolatry.

The people learned that being uncovered is a place of *iniquity*

What is iniquity? It is being *out of line* with God. The word used in the Bible really means "crookedness." It is from this concept that people say that they hope that a crook will go straight, once he has served his sentence. When we are not fully under God's covering, there is a spiritual distortion in our lives which is not only harmful to us, but can make us more vulnerable to trip up and sin in our personal walk. This tendency to stumble can be the result of our own sin or even the sin of others. We noted previously that the sin of parents often causes children to stumble. Jesus sees this as very serious:

> *"Whoever causes one of these little ones who believe to stumble, it would be better for him if, with a heavy millstone hung around his neck, he had been cast into the sea."*

> (Mark 9:42)

God's law, concerning iniquity visited down family lines, is very important to ponder for a moment. It tells us that our lives can be spiritually out of line with God, not just because of our own sin, but through the sin of those in the family who have come before us. As a result of their sinfulness or godliness, our forebears have had an effect on the spiritual condition of our lives. They have either added to our exposure or they have added to our protection.

At Ellel Ministries centers, we see many examples of people's lives being affected by the ungodliness of their forebears. There are frequently patterns of sin, disorder and disease running in families. We are *all* part of families. God's protective covering over our lives has been affected by the order or disorder which has occurred in our family. Later we will look some more at how iniquity affects people and even the land they occupy.

The people learned that God always has a recovery plan

Thankfully God had further instructions for His people in their place of iniquity. Amazingly, He has always been there at the bottom of the spiritual cliff to offer restoration to those who have fallen. In God's description of the rescue process, we find the use of the same Hebrew word which was part of the instruction to Noah, who was told to waterproof his boat. You may remember that the Bible used the Hebrew word *kaphar*, meaning "to cover," but it is also translated "to make atonement." How interesting that God's response to the people's iniquity was that they needed to get under cover – His cover!

For the Children of Israel, God ordained a special day of atonement, which would be set aside each year to give them the opportunity to come back under God's covenant protection. From this same Hebrew word, Jewish people today call it Yom Kippur – the day of cover. The instructions or commands were very specific and of course involved the shedding of sacrificial blood. God also made a way for all the damage, which had been caused by their disobedience, to be repaired. All the iniquity or distortion in people's lives could be taken away by a scapegoat:

> *"Then Aaron shall lay both of his hands on the head of the live goat, and confess over it all the iniquities of the sons of Israel . . . The goat shall bear on itself all their iniquities to a solitary land; and he shall release the goat in the wilderness."*

> (Leviticus 16:21–22)

Once again we are reminded that when God's covering is restored in the lives of His people, then His healing is available for the effects of their exposure. When we come indoors out of torrential rain, how wonderful it is to feel our bodies getting warm and dry again. Our God is a perfect Dad who wants to wrap us up as we come back into His house. In fact this does not just describe what God does, but we discover that this response to re-cover us simply demonstrates His unchangeable character. He made a covenant with His people to care for them and He will never break it.

What was a covenant in the time of the Bible?

When individuals, families or tribes saw an opportunity to make a beneficial agreement with their neighbors, they often established this relationship in the form of a covenant. It was a binding obligation between two parties (usually one stronger and one weaker), frequently sealed by bloodshed (to demonstrate the life and death nature of a covenant), and it included sacred vows. The purpose was to create a relationship in which each party was bound by specific undertakings to the other. The parties placed themselves under divine retribution (through an oath or swearing) should they attempt to avoid those undertakings. Such a covenant was usually only terminated by death. It was often sealed with the sharing of a meal.

In summary, covenants usually included:

- rituals enacted to symbolize the serious nature of the agreement;
- the making of unbreakable vows or promises;
- the invoking of divine witness and judgment.

By contrast, contracts are simply a way of exchanging material goods and labor. A covenant is totally different and involves the exchange of lives. It was this form of relationship which God established with His people, a divine alliance based on unconditional love. God undertook to care for them as they followed His instructions. He cannot break this promise!

The Old Covenant was specifically for the Jewish nation, the descendants of Abraham. Through Christ Jesus, the New Covenant reaches further to all mankind. In Galatians 3:29 Paul assures us:

> *And if you belong to Christ, then you are Abraham's descendants, heirs according to the promise.*

God regards those who belong to Jesus as family, and an offer is now open to all who believe in Him:

> *But as many as received Him, to them He gave the right to become children of God, even to those who believe in His name.*
>
> (John 1:12)

God's people learned about covenant and covering through marriage

God taught His people about covenant as He explained the significance of marriage, as well as the painful consequence of adultery. When children grow up and leave home to get married, this changes the order within a family. The new bride and groom must leave the shelter of their respective parents and begin a new family. Jesus said,

> *"For this reason a man shall leave his father and mother and be joined to his wife, and the two shall become one flesh."*
>
> (Matthew 19:5)

This is an opportunity for God's covering to be established in a new way over their lives and over the children that may come from their union.

The Bible refers to this relationship as a covenant and it is clear that this is a very deep and spiritual joining of a man and a woman. It is a covenant which the Lord regards as sacred:

> . . . *the* LORD *has been a witness between you and the wife of your youth, against whom you have dealt treacherously, though she is your companion and your wife by covenant.*

(Malachi 2:14b)

The marriage covenant is a place of God's covering for a man, for his wife and, in time, for their children. We see this so well described in the book of Ruth. She lost her husband through death and found a place of security in following her mother-in-law Naomi, who was a godly woman of wisdom. Returning from Moab to Bethlehem, there was no food for them to eat, so Ruth went to the fields of Naomi's kinsman to glean the grain which had been left during the harvesting. The owner, Boaz, noticed Ruth and, being aware of her vulnerability without a husband, he encouraged her to glean within the boundaries of his land and the protection that this would afford.

Naomi recognized the hand of God on Ruth and advised that she put herself into a situation in which she was dependent on the integrity of Boaz, even lying at his feet in the middle of the night. When he woke, Ruth was at the mercy of his protection.

> *He [Boaz] said, "Who are you?" And she answered, "I am Ruth your maid. So spread your [protective] covering over your maid, for you are a close relative."*

(Ruth 3:9)

Naomi had been right to encourage Ruth to trust Boaz. He was indeed a man of integrity, and he sought to bring Ruth and Naomi into a rightful place of order and security. The story of Ruth describes someone exposed by the circumstances of life, but restored into a place of God's covering, on this occasion through a covenant of marriage.

Like Ruth, we sometimes have to take difficult steps of faith, outside the apparent comfort of a familiar lifestyle, in order to seek the very best of God's covering for our lives. There is a well-known saying: "Better the devil we know." Guess who is spreading that lie! Thank You, Father God, that You tell the truth and that You are faithful to the covenant which You have made with us.

God's people learned that adultery brings spiritual exposure

God always gives choice to His people. They can follow His commands and benefit from His laws or they can go their own way. God's desire for true relationship with His people means that they must be free to choose to love Him or reject Him. When they spurn His love and seek the protection of other nations and their gods, it is betrayal to the covenant which God has offered to them. When men and women submit their lives to false gods they are spiritually uncovering their bodies every bit as much as they would in an act of sexual adultery. Both types of betrayal are very destructive. In the case of the nation of Israel, it resulted in their being overcome by their enemies and many being taken into exile:

> "Therefore, I gave her into the hand of her lovers, into the hand of the Assyrians, after whom she lusted. They uncovered her nakedness; they took her sons and daughters, but they slew her with the sword . . .
>
> (Ezekiel 23:9–10)

However much God yearned for His people to be in covenant with Him, He had to release them to choose. A lover who is held under control is not truly able to love. The enemy is very seductive in enticing people into his sphere of influence. False gods or adulterous lovers can seem a very attractive shelter when life is too challenging. However, the enemy's "covering" is never a place of freedom but always a net of captivity. He hides this truth from those whom he ensnares, but eventually the bondage becomes all too clear. Mercifully, God waits for His people to recognize their foolish alliances and He invites them to be in covenant with Him again.

God's people learned about the need of His forgiveness

We find that the word *kaphar*, meaning "to cover," is translated many times in the Bible as "to forgive." The two words are almost synonymous when we consider the way God deals with the sinfulness of His people. He sees the defilement of our lives and in His mercy He longs to cover the place of shame and to restore our dignity, just as the father did with the prodigal son when he returned home smeared with the filth of the pigs.

Only God can rightfully forgive, cover and cleanse our iniquity. The psalmist says:

> *O You who hear prayer,*
> *To You all men come.*
> *Iniquities prevail against me;*
> *As for our transgressions, You forgive [cover] them.*
>
> (Psalm 65:2–3)

Flesh wounds can fester when hidden under dirty bandages. In the same way, when we try to cover up our sinfulness, the issues remain in the dark and unresolved. Remarkably, when God forgives and covers our sin, everything is in the light, and cleansing can follow.

It is a fact that sins and wounds often remain covered up and unresolved in our lives. It is wonderful to see how God gently leads us, if we are willing to follow, through the process of re-establishing truth, light and healing. Every day, we have the privilege of seeing Him do this precious work at Ellel centers, as people respond to His touch. He is available anywhere to those who seek His forgiveness and restoration. The cost of this recovery was the cross, the only place where God's justice could be satisfied.

God's people needed to know that He alone had a final and perfect plan for covering

Through the prophets, not least through the remarkable words of Isaiah, God revealed to His people that there was a perfect plan prepared for mankind. A Savior would come bearing the anointing of God with good news of restoration from our brokenness and our spiritual captivity. Instead of the covering of darkness and heaviness that surrounds people's lives, the Savior would bring a new spiritual garment of light and rejoicing.

Isaiah foresees the coming of One who will walk in perfect obedience to the Father, re-establishing covenant and restoring joy under God's mantle of freedom from the enemy's oppressive hold:

> *The Spirit of the* Lord *God is upon me,*
> *Because the* Lord *has anointed me*
> *To bring good news to the afflicted;*
> *He has sent me to bind up the brokenhearted,*
> *To proclaim liberty to captives*
> *And freedom to prisoners:*
> *To proclaim the favorable year of the* Lord
> *And the day of vengeance of our God;*
> *To comfort all who mourn,*
> *To grant those who mourn in Zion,*
> *Giving them a garland instead of ashes,*
> *The oil of gladness instead of mourning,*
> *The mantle of praise instead of a spirit of fainting.*
>
> (Isaiah 61:1–3)

In Luke chapter 4, we see Jesus standing up in the synagogue, reading from Isaiah and announcing that He is the One about whom Isaiah had spoken. Jesus is the fulfillment of all the promises which God has made. He has promised to restore man back into the protection and blessing of a covenant relationship with Him. Jesus is ultimate covering!

Understanding the full benefit of God's covering

We can choose to abide in Jesus or ignore Him, but we cannot make an informed choice without a knowledge of the consequence of those choices. God gives an understanding of the benefits of His covering throughout the Bible, but nowhere more succinctly than in Psalm 91.

The psalm begins by clearly stating that God's covering is a place which protects us from an unseen hostile realm which can harm us, like the desert sun.

> *He who dwells in the shelter of the Most High*
> *Will abide in the shadow of the Almighty.*
> *I will say to the* LORD, *"My refuge and my fortress,*
> *My God in whom I trust!"*

(vv. 1–2)

The Hebrew word for "shelter" literally means a place of cover. Interestingly the translation of this word in the Lutheran Bible is associated with the word "umbrella." The shade of a parasol can be lifesaving under a burning sun.

To enter into this place of God's covering means release from the captivity of the ruler of this world.

> *For it is He who delivers you from the snare of the trapper*
> *And from the deadly pestilence.*

(v. 3)

The enemy brings entrapment, death and destruction, not abundant life.

God's covering shields us from attack.

> *He will cover you with His pinions [feathers],*
> *And under His wings you may seek refuge;*
> *His faithfulness is a shield and bulwark.*

(v. 4)

God is not passive in the protection of His children.

In the safety of this protection and security, fear has no place, whatever the enemy throws at us or however he tries to intimidate.

> *You will not be afraid of the terror by night,*
> *Or of the arrow that flies by day;*
> *Of the pestilence that stalks in the darkness,*
> *Or of the destruction that lays waste at noon.*

(vv. 5–6)

The enemy is a terrorist, seeking to control our lives through fear.

Many will refuse the covenant protection of God. We can only watch and be saddened at the choice which they have made and the consequence of that rebellion.

> *A thousand may fall at your side*
> *And ten thousand at your right hand,*
> *But it shall not approach you.*
> *You will only look on with your eyes*
> *And see the recompense of the wicked.*
> *For you have made the LORD, my refuge,*
> *Even the Most High, your dwelling place.*
> *No evil will befall you,*
> *Nor will any plague come near your tent.*

(vv. 7–10)

We can boldly declare to the world that God is the protector of those who love Him.

There is angelic help for those who walk in God's covering.

> *For He will give His angels charge concerning you,*
> *To guard you in all your ways.*
> *They will bear you up in their hands,*
> *That you do not strike your foot against a stone.*

(vv. 11–12)

So many times when praying for people who have experienced traumatic accidents, I have heard them say, "There must have been angels,
because I cannot see how I managed to come out alive." We live in
an evil and hostile world, full of accidents and violence, which are
the consequence of the rebellion of mankind. God longs to see His
children walking in His safety.

Under God's covering, we are no longer subject to the enemy's
control, but in a place of spiritual authority above all the powers of
darkness.

> *You will tread upon the lion and the cobra,*
> *The young lion and the serpent you will trample down.*
> *Because he has loved Me, therefore I will deliver him;*
> *I will set him securely on high, because he has known*
>   *My name.*

(vv. 13–14)

This promise from the Old Testament becomes a daily reality for
disciples of Jesus, when they walk in obedience to His instructions.
It reminds us of Jesus' words:

> *"Behold, I have given you authority to tread on serpents and scorpions,*
> *and over all the power of the enemy, and nothing will injure you."*

(Luke 10:19)

In the intimacy of God's covering, there need be no barrier to
our communication with Him, especially when we are looking for
His help.

> *He will call upon Me, and I will answer him;*
> *I will be with him in trouble; I will rescue him and*
>   *honor him.*

(v. 15)

To summarize, God's covering is clearly good for our spiritual,
emotional and physical well-being.

With a long life I will satisfy him
And let him see My salvation.

(v. 16)

This psalm inevitably leaves us with questions about God's cover-ing over our own lives and how much we, and those who have been responsible for us, have walked in obedience to God's commands. Thankfully, God is always ready to respond to these questions and to restore His shelter.

The enemy hates to see God's plan for covering

It is worth noting that some verses from Psalm 91 were used by Satan in an attempt to draw Jesus under his dark spiritual authority. The devil hates to see the protection, described in this psalm, afforded to those who walk in obedience to Father God. In the tempting of Jesus in the wilderness, Satan does all he can to persuade Jesus to disobey His Father's instructions. He even twists Scripture to encourage Jesus to presume on the Father's protection, irrespective of obedience.

> *And he [the devil] led Him [Jesus] to Jerusalem and had Him stand on the pinnacle of the temple, and said to Him, "If You are the Son of God, throw Yourself down from here; for it is written, 'He will command His angels concerning You to guard You,' and 'On their hands they will bear You up, so that You will not strike Your foot against a stone.'" And Jesus answered and said to him, "It is said, 'You shall not put the Lord Your God to the test.'"*

(Luke 4:9–12)

How interesting that Satan should choose to quote these words from Psalm 91, when addressing Jesus, bearing in mind the next verse in that psalm.

> *You will tread upon the lion and the cobra, the young lion and the serpent you will trample down.*

(v. 13)

In this psalm about God's covering we are being clearly told of the authority, in Christ, which we have over Satan, and all the powers of darkness. In this world there is a battle for spiritual authority and, like Jesus in the wilderness, we determine that spiritual authority and covering over our lives by our choices. We can follow what the ruler of this world (Satan) says, or follow the Creator of the world revealed through Christ Jesus. We decide who has the upper hand in our lives!

Having been defeated in the wilderness, Satan was still determined to expose and destroy the authority of Jesus. He continued to look for those who would join his rebellion against the Son of God and he found plenty of support. Even the soldiers took pleasure in stripping Jesus of His clothes, to mock Him and shame Him with a garment which would make Him look like an earthly king.

> *They stripped Him and put a scarlet robe on Him. And after twisting together a crown of thorns, they put it on His head, and a reed in His right hand; and they knelt down before Him, saying, "Hail, King of the Jews!"*
>
> (Matthew 27:28–29)

It is typical of the enemy's tactics to take any opportunity to undermine the spiritual covering and dignity which God has made available for those who love Him. If we remain dependent on the faithfulness of God, all the enemy's attempts to destroy our inheritance and destiny will come to nothing.

Summary

Following man's rebellion in the Garden, Father God had a plan to restore a covenant relationship with a particular people, called to be His children. Having chosen to seek the wisdom of this world, and its ruler (Satan), man began a long journey of rediscovering the importance of God's foundational laws. God's people needed to learn how they could once again know the protection and provision of their Father in heaven. They had to learn that His covenant promises could only be enjoyed by those who trusted Him, obeyed His commands and ordered their life in God's way.

The word "atonement," which the Bible uses to describe the process of getting right with God, actually means "to cover." God's people needed to understand that covenant, forgiveness and covering are inseparable. Throughout the Old Testament the benefit of God's covering was explained to, and experienced by, the children of Israel. All the time God was pointing towards the perfect solution which would come through His Son Jesus, the Anointed One, the only person who would ever walk this earth and fully obey the commands of God.

Jesus would be a perfect representative of man before God and a perfect representative of God to man. He would call Himself Son of Man and Son of God and renew the divine covenant with mankind. Jesus understood and obeyed God's law and God's order.

CHAPTER 5

Covering through God's order

Living under a strong umbrella

God's heart for the widow and the orphan

The well-known Bible teacher talked quietly, but determinedly, as he addressed the delegates. Derek Prince was speaking at an international conference for Ellel Ministries called *Let the Oppressed Go Free*. As he sat on the stage, we all sensed the extraordinary opportunity which God had given us to listen to this true elder of the Church. It turned out to be the last major conference at which Derek spoke before he died. He was insistent that, despite all the wonderful truths about God which he had discovered through many years of seeking Him, the essence of following Jesus was summed up in words written by the apostle James:

> *Pure and undefiled religion in the sight of our God and Father is this: to visit orphans and widows in their distress, and to keep oneself unstained by the world.*
>
> (James 1:27)

That verse was unexpected. The delegates had poised themselves to discover Derek's view on the meaning of life. But as he clearly and simply expounded the truth within this verse, we realized that we were touching the very heart of God. Since that time, I have continued to ponder the reason why this verse, as with scores of others within the Bible (e.g. Exodus 22:22, "You shall not afflict any widow or orphan"), should so specifically highlight the needs of orphans and widows. It is now clear to me that orphans and widows represent those who have lost a foundational means of covering which God wants mankind to have. Godly order within a family group is His primary way of protecting His people.

Whatever personal circumstances have led to the loss of a husband or parents, the consequence for the family is a loss of vital spiritual safety. God has declared that He will not leave this exposure unresolved and, in relationship with Him, we must pursue justice. He commands His people:

> *Learn to do good;*
> *Seek justice,*
> *Reprove the ruthless,*
> *Defend the orphan,*
> *Plead for the widow.*

(Isaiah 1:17)

Sometimes on television we see pictures of naked frightened children exposed to the horrors of a war-torn environment. From my heart comes a desperate, if impractical, desire to scoop them up into my arms and offer a place of protection and comfort. When we feel like this, we are expressing the same emotion that God feels as He sees the hostile spiritual darkness which surrounds people who've become separated from His covering.

Jesus explains to His disciples one day that He will not be with them for much longer. He knows that, alongside Him, they had experienced a sense of security and fathering which had been life changing for them. He expresses the heart of His Father as He tells them that the Holy Spirit will continue to watch over them, as they follow His commands with child-like faith:

> *"I will ask the Father, and He will give you another Helper, that He may be with you forever; that is the Spirit of truth, whom the world*

cannot receive, because it does not see Him or know Him, but you know Him because He abides with you and will be in you. I will not leave you as orphans; I will come to you."

(John 14:16–18)

Being right with God . . . through godly order

In God's eyes we are unique individuals but we are also part of a precious body of people whom He sees as His family. The spiritual covering of our lives, as adults, depends primarily on our personal walk with God. However, the reality of our interdependence with other people means that this covering, throughout our lives, is very much affected by those around us. This will be particularly significant with those who have a directive or protective role over our lives. It is most critical when we are young children, very dependent upon the integrity of our parents. Even as adults, other people at work, in church, in local and national governments are making decisions which affect our well-being. These decisions, godly or ungodly, can significantly affect the physical and spiritual safety of our lives. With this in mind, we would do well to spend time praying for them rather than criticizing them. The solution for repairing the spiritual cover over our lives, when leaders sin, is to forgive them and, if appropriate, sensitively confront them with what we believe to be God's truth.

In our relationships with one another, God has ordained structures which maintain right order and spiritual authority, so that these can be a means of His covering. Even within the Godhead there had to be order so that the purposes of God could be fulfilled. Paul describes this basic principle of order as it comes through the Godhead into human families on earth:

> *But I want you to understand that Christ is the head of every man, and the man is the head of a woman, and God is the head of Christ.*
>
> (1 Corinthians 11:3)

Jesus is entirely equal with the Father but still there needed to be a divine protocol for the purposes of God to be fulfilled. Writing in

Philippians 2:5–7 Paul encourages believers to emulate the attitude of Christ:

> *Have this attitude in yourselves which was also in Christ Jesus, who, although He existed in the form of God, did not regard equality with God a thing to be grasped, but emptied Himself, taking the form of a bond-servant, and being made in the likeness of men.*

This order is the way God's protection and provision is maintained. Men and women are entirely equal before God but He asks them also to walk according to His order so as to allow His purposes.

We need to explore within the Bible what God means by His *law and order*. The Wild West made a wonderful back-drop for cowboy films but most people only truly feel safe where there *is* law and order. God has made a place of spiritual safety through His foundational laws and also by showing us the order for our lives and relationships, an order which brings well-being for everyone. What are the structures for godly relationships so that God's divine order and covering are in place?

God covers through those He calls to be leaders

Sheep need a shepherd to lead them to safe grazing. The shepherd weighs up the situation regarding food supply, safety from hazards and the threat of wild animals, and he then directs the sheep to the place which is best for them.

Throughout the Bible, God provided for and protected His people through leaders who were willing to walk in obedience to His commands. God shielded the children of Israel, from the famine that was threatening them, through the obedience of Joseph, who looking back over the events of his life was able to say:

> *"God sent me before you to preserve for you a remnant in the earth, and to keep you alive by a great deliverance."*

(Genesis 45:7)

Through the obedience of Hezekiah, God brought recovery to Israel from the devastation of the land and the people:

> *Hezekiah became King when he was twenty-five years old; and he reigned twenty-nine years in Jerusalem . . . He did right in the sight of the* LORD *. . . So the* LORD *heard Hezekiah and healed the people.*
>
> (2 Chronicles 29:1, 2 & 30:20)

Leviticus 16:6 makes clear that the head of a household carries particular responsibility to walk in godliness, not just for his own sake, but also to be a means of God's covering for the whole of the extended family living within the same home:

> *Then Aaron shall offer the bull for the sin offering which is for himself, that he may make atonement for himself and for his household.*

Some are called to carry that responsibility further, representing members of a tribe or a nation. God gave Aaron, his family and the Levites a special role as priests, to be a means of God's covering for all the sons of Israel:

> *"I have given the Levites as a gift to Aaron and to his sons from among the sons of Israel, to perform the service of the sons of Israel at the tent of meeting and to make atonement [a covering] on behalf of the sons of Israel . . . "*
>
> (Numbers 8:19)

We serve a God of order and when that order is respected we find ourselves enjoying His covenant and covering.

People need a leader to give direction, not to take control! God has always provided leaders, even though they, and those they lead, have not been perfect. We need leaders in our nations, our communities, our households and our families to make right decisions on our behalf. The godliness of those leaders will have a very significant effect on the physical and spiritual well-being of those they are leading, especially where the members of the group are immature or unable to stand up for themselves.

We see this very clearly in the story of the centurion who sought healing for his servant from Jesus. This godly Roman officer understood the principles of military structure. He recognized the godly authority invested in Jesus and he also understood the responsibility which he personally carried for his servant:

> " . . . *for this reason I [the centurion] did not even consider myself worthy to come to You [Jesus], but just say the word, and my servant will be healed."*
>
> (Luke 7:7)

Of course the result was healing for the slave, through the godly order evident in this household. The petition of the centurion was a means of God's covering and restoration for a servant who had very few rights of his own.

God has provided leaders in the Body of Christ to carry a specific mantle of spiritual authority and responsibility for the well-being of His people. They hold, as it were, a significant umbrella of God's covering over the people. The primary task of a leader is to declare *direction*. This is what we see the apostle James doing in Acts 15:

> *After they had stopped speaking, James answered, saying, "Brethren, listen to me . . . it is my judgment that we do not trouble those who are turning to God from among the Gentiles . . . "*
>
> (vv. 13, 19)

Leadership is a very necessary role, but we are actually dependent on the gifting and godliness of *all* of the members of the Body, in order to have God's full covering.

It is essential for a ship to have a captain, and not a committee, in order to give direction, but it will be an extremely unsafe ship if the captain ignores his crew and all the vital skills which they bring.

God gives the picture of a shepherd

Every group of people needs more than just a leader. We need shepherds. The picture of a shepherd appears throughout the Bible to explain how God wants to lead, protect and nurture His people. David was a mighty King but he was also the shepherd whom God chose for His people: "And the LORD said to you, 'You will shepherd My people Israel, and you will be a ruler over Israel'" (2 Samuel 5:2b).

How interesting that Jesus commissions Peter with similar words:

> He [Jesus] said to him a second time, "Simon, son of John, do you love Me?" He said to Him, "Yes, Lord; You know that I love You." He said to him, "Shepherd My sheep."
>
> (John 21:16)

Shepherding is not a calling which is established through self-importance, but through self-surrender.

The principle of shepherding is key to understanding God's way of covering His children. Of course Jesus is *the* Good Shepherd. God's direction, protection and nurture for our lives all depend on Him, but there will always be a need for under-shepherds to be a means of God's covering. Unfortunately the godly principle of shepherding has been spoiled for many people who have experienced "heavy shepherding." This has been a source of crushing rather than feeding.

A godly shepherd directs without controlling. He protects the sheep by exercising strength, without demanding status. He nurtures the sheep with godly wisdom rather than human intellect. No one person will be fully gifted in all these qualities, so the Holy Spirit distributes these abilities amongst the human shepherds. Godly shepherds will increasingly develop the character of Jesus.

Of course shepherds do not always do a good job. Because of wounded-ness, selfishness, apathy or insecurity, shepherds can sometimes do more harm than good. Ezekiel chapter 34 makes very clear God's view concerning those who have not cared for the sheep as He intended:

> "Son of man, prophesy against the shepherds of Israel. Prophesy and say to those shepherds, 'Thus says the Lord GOD, "Woe, shepherds of Israel who have been feeding themselves! Should not the shepherds feed the flock?"'"

> (Ezekiel 34:2)

God does not say that the principle of shepherding is wrong: He simply says that there are some bad shepherds!

I remember a lady we will call Paula, telling me how, as a young Christian some years previously, she had been very troubled by a directive personal prophecy. It had been given to her by a forceful speaker who was visiting her church. She had felt very exposed and had desperately needed the guidance of the leader of the church, but he had casually dismissed her request for help.

As we spoke, Paula was gradually able to forgive him for not being the provider of God's protection and direction. The Lord then brought significant healing to the place of fear and confusion which had remained unresolved within her. Although forgiving the one who had given the prophecy was also important, it was forgiving the leader that was more difficult for her. This shepherd had not properly guarded his sheep on that particular day.

Covered through godly submission to one another

We are made for relationship, both with God and with each other. When our relationships are right with God, this brings a further aspect of spiritual covering over our lives – a "corporate" covering. This gives us supernatural authority and power to fulfill together God's plans and purposes in a needy world. The psalmist gives a remarkable picture of this spiritual covering:

Behold how good and how pleasant it is
For brothers to dwell together in unity!
It is like the precious oil upon the head,
Coming down upon the beard,
Even Aaron's beard,
Coming down upon the edge of his robes.
It is like the dew of Hermon
Coming down upon the mountains of Zion;
For there the Lord commanded the blessing – life forever.

(Psalm 133)

God has established a principle for Christian relationships which is very different from how the world operates. It can be stated like this: there is safety and strength in the Body of Christ when we recognize the anointing of God on one another and when we are in mutual submission to that godly authority in each person. The Spirit of God enables the Body of Christ to move corporately in God's purposes by gifting and equipping the individual members in different ways. The apostle Paul explains:

For just as we have many members in one body and all the members
do not have the same function, so we, who are many, are one body in
Christ, and individually members one of another.

(Romans 12:4–5)

If we let Him, the Holy Spirit will bring order, direction, protection and nurture into God's family. He does this by equipping some to lead, some to teach, some to minister healing, some to prophesy, etc. Together God can cover and shepherd us through the gifting which He distributes. As we recognize this and let Christ have His way in us, and in others, we will know His corporate and individual covering and blessing. Paul states this principle very simply:

be subject to one another in the fear of Christ.

(Ephesians 5:21)

Covered through the order of godly parenting

There is no more significant place for the presence or absence of God's covering than the relationship between small children and their parents. Mothers and fathers have complementary roles. Mothers tend towards providing the unconditional love and nurture, whereas fathers tend towards the protection and affirmation of each member of the family. Fathers are called to hold a very important umbrella over the family, but the book of Proverbs reminds us that godly mothers are also essential for the well-being of the household:

> *An excellent wife, who can find her?*
> *For her worth is far above jewels . . .*
> *She is not afraid of the snow for her household,*
> *For all her household are clothed with scarlet.*
>
> (Proverbs 31:10, 21)

Throughout the Bible, God emphasizes the immense significance of the parent-child relationship. Even the divine order within the Godhead demonstrates the importance of this God-designed relationship. Obeying His Father provided safety for Jesus as He came into, and walked through, the spiritual hostility of this earth. For every human being, this crucial relationship between parent and child was intended by God to provide the principal means of His covering. As we grow from the innocence of childhood to the maturity of adulthood, we should move from total dependence on our parents to full personal accountability.

For each of us during our early lives, the family is the basic structure for the establishing of godly order and covering around us. God intended that a father and a mother, in right relationship with each other and with their children, would provide a safe structure for the godly shelter and well-being of the whole family. According to the fifth commandment, honoring our parents even extends our life on earth:

"Honor your father and mother, that your days may be prolonged in the land which the LORD your God gives you."

(Exodus 20:12)

Of course this is not a perfect world and God knows that much family life is very far from what He has purposed. God does not condemn those whose experience of life was not lived in the right ways He planned for families. He is our Redeemer, but it is important to realize that, where lives have been outside godly order, there will inevitably be a consequence. At Ellel Ministries centers, we have ministered to countless people who have described their childhood as basically *unsafe*. They may not have been overtly abused but they are simply expressing the lack of safe godly cover within the family, usually because of parental absence or conflict.

Parents have often tried their best to provide a good home but through their own history of wounding, they have been unable to function as God intended. As we look back, my wife and I see very clearly now how far short we were from God's right way of parenting. We loved our children but we were responsible for many gaps in their covering. Wonderfully, God can redeem, recover and heal the anxieties and wounding caused by any lack of right spiritual protection. He can do it today. Psalm 27:10 promises:

For my father and my mother have forsaken me,
But the LORD will take me up.

God is plainly telling us here that, where parents have failed, He will cover us!

A picture of parental cover

The principles of God's covering are, of course, best discovered through God's Word, but occasionally we stumble across a confirmation of the reality of Scripture in the most unlikely circumstances.

My wife and I were at a Christian summer camp some while ago and we were asked to talk to a young man who had been involved in the occult, but had recently accepted Jesus as his Lord. During the conversation we talked about some of the occult powers which he had developed, including his ability to constantly "see" into the spiritual realms. He was very keen for these un-godly powers to be cleansed and to receive only those safe spiritual gifts which God wanted to impart to him.

He explained that, even while on the camp, he was able to "see" things which were troubling for him. He went on to explain, "I can see families where there is a sort of canopy which extends out from the parents over the children. The enemy seems angry that they are protected and safe. But there are other families where things do not seem right, and the canopy is damaged or missing altogether. I don't understand this," he said, "but I feel very troubled for the children who don't have this canopy over them."

We did our best to explain the principle of God's covering in families. We advised him that, although his ability to always "see" in this way was probably not one which God wanted to continue, he had actually caught a glimpse of just how important the godliness of parents was to the spiritual well-being of children.

Our heavenly Father is the ultimate parent, releasing His character into godly families. However old we are, we will always be His children and we will never stop needing Him. The enemy is a false father, holding many men and women who have ignored the truth of Jesus in his deceptive ways. Speaking to His own people who claimed to have God as their Father, Jesus said,

> *"You are of your father the devil, and you want to do the desires of your father. He was a murderer from the beginning, and does not stand in the truth because there is no truth in him. Whenever he speaks a lie, he speaks from his own nature, for he is a liar and the father of lies."*

(John 8:44)

Covered through the order of godly inheritance

God has not just made His covenant with individuals: He has also made this wonderful promise to families and their descendants. This was clearly expressed to Abraham:

> *"I will establish My covenant between Me and you and your descendants after you throughout their generations for an everlasting covenant, to be God to you and your descendants after you."*

(Genesis 17:7)

God has purposed a godly inheritance for His people. Parents are intended to bring blessing into that inheritance through their godly behavior and teaching. This has always been God's plan for families, as we can see from Genesis 18:19 where, speaking about Abraham, He says,

> *"For I have chosen him, so that he may command his children and his household after him to keep the way of the LORD by doing righteousness and justice, so that the LORD may bring upon Abraham what He has spoken about him."*

Many Jewish men wear a small skull cap, which they call a *Kippah*. The name comes from the same Hebrew word which, as we have previously seen, is used in the Bible to mean "covering," "forgiveness" and "atonement." The cap is a symbol of the inheritance of God's covering which He has promised the children of Israel.

We all have a past family heritage. We have inherited either spiritual protection or exposure in our lives, depending on the godliness or otherwise of our forebears. Deuteronomy 7:9 says:

> *"Know therefore that the LORD your God, He is God, the faithful God, who keeps His covenant and His lovingkindness to a thousandth generation with those who love Him and keep His commandments . . ."*

God is absolutely faithful to His promise for the family line of His people, but they have constantly broken the terms of this covenant. As Exodus 20:5–6 makes clear, the consequence is a distorted inheritance which can leave us spiritually exposed:

> *"You shall not worship them [idols] or serve them; for I, the* LORD *your God, am a jealous God, visiting the iniquity of the fathers on the children, on the third and the fourth generation of those who hate Me . . . "*

We saw previously that the word "iniquity" describes spiritual crookedness or distortion, which is the condition of people's lives where God's covering is not fully in place. Spiritual exposure in the family can put us out of line with God and His desired blessing for our lives. We will look later at God's remedy

Covered through the order of godly marriage

When a woman enters into marriage, she agrees to participate in a new structure of relationship for God's covering of her life. She was not uncovered as a single woman, because godly relationships which existed with family and friends provided the order which gave her spiritual safety. However, when entering the covenant of marriage, God's new order in her life requires her willingness to be in rightful submission to her husband. Similarly her husband is required to give his life in a sacrificial way for her protection, thus bringing God's covering both to the marriage and to their individual lives. Teaching on this principle, Paul writes:

> *Wives, be subject to your own husbands as to the Lord . . . Husbands, love your wives, just as Christ also loved the church and gave Himself up for her.*
>
> (Ephesians 5:22, 25)

Both the husband and the wife experience a new place of God's direction, protection and nurture as they enter into the covenant of marriage. In a traditional Jewish wedding service, the couple make their vows to each other under a prayer shawl erected as a canopy held up on four poles. Their new union is being publicly declared to be the new place of God's covering.

We saw previously in the book of Ruth how God works in the lives of those who truly seek Him, to restore rightful covering. Having lost her husband, Ruth chooses to follow the godly leading of Naomi, her mother-in-law. This provides a place of safety for her, but God has an even better plan of redemption. Ruth's gentle obedience to Naomi's directions culminates in her being restored into an amazing place of God's protection through Naomi's relative, Boaz.

To arrive at this, she has to take a huge step of faith in following the advice of Naomi, submitting herself to Boaz, not at all certain of his response. As she lies at his feet, she asks for his covering and, because he regards her as a woman of integrity, he responds even beyond the need of that moment by offering her a covenant of marriage.

Marriage is a huge step in anyone's life. It is a place where God asks us to give our lives into a vulnerable relationship of trust. If we do this, recognizing how God views this important covenant, He Himself is there to provide the protection. This makes our vulnerability a safe step to take. Men and women are equal before God, in the same way that Jesus is equal to the Father. However, just as Jesus chose to walk in submission to the Father, so too does God call the woman to choose to walk in submission to her husband. When this choice is freely made, and the husband also gives himself in sacrificial love to his wife, God's order and His covering are in place.

In this spiritually hostile world, God has ordained marriage and family to be the foundational way by which mankind finds protection and nurture. The godly leading (or headship) of a loving husband establishes a rightful structure which guards the whole family. Because of the nature of this fallen world, many marriages are destroyed by sickness, death and sinful behavior. This loss of spiritual and physical protection, as families disintegrate, grieves the heart of God. We saw earlier the special place which God has in His heart for those who have been widowed or orphaned, whatever the cause. He is the perfect Redeemer and He knows the best way to restore the damage caused by family breakdown.

What about those who are not married?

Let's be very clear, single people are no less under God's covering than those who are married, provided that they seek to live in right relationship with Him and those around them. Marriage is an important and particular structure of relationship, but every one of us interacts with colleagues, friends and relatives, Christian or otherwise. Some people are in places of leadership, some in support, some giving counsel and some offering practical skills. Essentially, it is godly order which gives us God's covering, not our ability to find a particular human protector.

God is our shelter when we walk in His ways and when we submit to one another as He directs. We are spiritually exposed when we choose to disregard His order. For example, partnerships where there is sexual intimacy, other than within the marriage covenant of a man and a woman, are not in God's order and do not bring His covering. Nothing stops His love for us but there is much that we do to stop His blessing, if we so choose.

Same sex partnerships do not provide a safe place for God's covering for either the couple or for children. There are many reasons, usually through damage to their human identity, why some people find comfort in intimate relationships with people of the same sex. However, this is not God's order. These desires are a distortion of that order, coming from places of wounding which need understanding and healing. To endorse and promote these desires as being a created sexual orientation simply increases the distortion and the resulting dysfunction.

Covered through godly order in our personal lives

Apart from these issues of relationships, we all have a personal responsibility to conduct our lives in such a way as to place ourselves under God's protection. When we sin, our lives become spiritually distorted. We have seen that the Bible calls this iniquity and it means being out of line with God. Where we are not in line with God, we move outside His covering. On a day of hailstorms, children who are jumping in and out of the shelter of dad's umbrella will get wet and cold. Iniquity damages lives.

Through His instructions about order, God has provided the ways which will shelter us under His spiritual umbrella. He does not remove this protection but we always have a choice to stay under cover or to go our separate ways: "But your iniquities have made a separation between you and your God" (Isaiah 59:2).

God has created us with a spirit, a soul (mind, will and emotions) and a body, and He is seeking to restore these to wholeness and freedom. Understanding this, at the end of the book of Thessalonians Paul prays:

> *Now may the God of peace Himself sanctify you entirely; and may your spirit, soul and body be preserved complete, without blame at the coming of our Lord Jesus Christ.*
>
> (1 Thessalonians 5:23)

We were designed to know God's wisdom (by His Spirit) in our human spirit and to make decisions in our soul which follow His ways rather than what the world says.

Children can very often know the voice of God more clearly than those who have allowed their worldly intellect to govern their decisions. Elihu, in the book of Job, puts it very well:

> *"But it is a spirit in man,*
> *And the breath of the Almighty gives them understanding.*
> *The abundant in years may not be wise,*
> *Nor may elders understand justice."*
>
> (Job 32:8–9)

God intended that, even within our own being, there would be His order. The Holy Spirit should rule over the human spirit in man.

Our spirit should rule over the soul, which then directs the physical body in accordance with the will of God. When this is out of order, through wounding or through sinful choices, the godly rule and covering within our body is affected and we are left exposed and vulnerable.

> *He that hath no rule over his spirit is like a city that is broken down, and without walls.*

(Proverbs 25:28 KJV)

Disorder and exposure in our lives can result from many issues. Today we can ask God to help us to understand the truth of what has happened and let His order be re-established, through confession and forgiveness. Even when we have been deeply hurt, we may need to consider our own responsibilities; this can be very hard.

God sees the disorder in our lives

Some while ago, I was talking to a Christian called Daniel. He had experienced some appalling sexual abuse as a little child and he explained how his life now felt exactly like a damaged city without walls. He seemed to be painfully sensitive to the emotional and spiritual influence of many situations which would not necessarily affect other people at all. As we talked, he began to realize just how terribly uncovered he had been as a child, through the carelessness of his parents and by abuse from a friend of the family.

What made the recall of events even worse for Daniel was that he had chosen, as a little boy of six, to secretly accept an ice cream from the man who had later abused him. He knew at the time that this was disobeying his parents. As he thought about the abuse, it seemed to him as if he had been tricked into opening a gate to an enemy, albeit with no understanding of what was happening. We explained that it was typical of this kind of abuser, who often sought to implicate the abused child with such choices. In this way they tried to make the child take some responsibility for the horror of the abuse. What a sickening twist of God's order. When the apostle Paul was confronted with a man who was seeking to confound God's purposes, he challenged him with the words:

> *"You who are full of all deceit and fraud, you son of the devil, you enemy of all righteousness, will you not cease to make crooked the straight ways of the Lord?"*

(Acts 13:10)

We reminded Daniel that Jesus speaks very strong words in the Bible against those who have caused little ones to stumble. Whilst realizing the gross sin of the abuser, Daniel still felt it right to acknowledge that he had stumbled in accepting the ice cream. He forgave himself and received God's forgiveness. He said it was as if he was able to now fully close the city gate of his life, and stop this access to the enemy, for the first time in forty years.

Over a number of prayer times, Daniel was gradually able to forgive the abuser and to forgive his own dad for not being aware of all that had happened. In a remarkable way, stone by stone, God built up the rightful spiritual walls around Daniel's life and he began to find a new sense of security and peace from all the inner terror that had gripped him for so long. It is by seeing God work in wonderful ways like this that I can confidently declare that God truly recovers and restores His children today!

When each one of us accepted Jesus as the Lord of our lives, the human spirit that is within us was brought from darkness into spiritual light and life, by the Holy Spirit. We began to "see" the truth of God in a completely new way as "The Spirit Himself testifies with our spirit that we are children of God" (Romans 8:16). Although our human spirit is now alive to God, we may well be carrying the damage of many years in darkness. The traumas of life affect us so deeply that even our human spirit can be crushed and broken.

Sometimes, as Scripture acknowledges, you can see the story of a person's life written on their face, reflecting the joys but also the pain of all that has happened:

> *A joyful heart makes a cheerful face,*
> *But when the heart is sad, the spirit is broken.*

(Proverbs 15:13)

We need healing in our human spirit (as we do in every part of our being) so that the order and covering of our personal lives can be restored.

God's order for the covering of land

Have you ever wondered why some places feel safer than others? Let's take a moment to see what the Bible says about God's covering over land as well as people. At the moment of the creation of man, God gave him authority to subdue the earth and occupy the land. Man's rebellion gave Satan an opportunity to usurp that authority, but God's plan has always been that His covering and peace would be over land where the occupants followed His commands:

> *"If you walk in My statutes and keep My commandments so as to carry them out . . . I shall also grant peace in the land, so that you may lie down with no one making you tremble. I shall also eliminate harmful beasts from the land, and no sword will pass through your land."*

(Leviticus 26:3, 6)

We have described God's covering as being like an umbrella or parasol. When a dad holds up a big umbrella over his family, it is worth noting that the ground which they are standing on also benefits from the same shelter. We can say that land is spiritually protected or exposed through the godliness or ungodliness of the occupants, particularly those in leadership. When the priest, under the Old Covenant, followed God's instructions on the Day of Atonement to restore the people, he was also instructed to make atonement (establish God's covering) for the ground and tent which was the place of meeting with God: "and make atonement for the holy sanctuary, and he [the priest] shall make atonement for the tent of meeting and for the altar" (Leviticus 16:33).

Ground which is spiritually clean returns a benefit to the occupants. The enemy promotes barrenness in people's lives and on this earth. It is hard to find shelter in a barren landscape. God seeks fruitfulness throughout His creation and, when ground is fruitful, it gives back the materials necessary for the physical covering of man. It was in fact God's first instruction to man, that he should be fruitful, which is all about demonstrating God's character on this earth: "God blessed them; and God said to them, 'Be fruitful and multiply . . . '" (Genesis 1:28).

From plants and trees we build houses and harvest food, the physical protection and provision for our lives. The relationship between man and the land he occupies has always been important to God. It is essential to the fullness of God's covering and to the covenant with His people. God promises:

> *"If they confess their iniquity . . . then I will remember My covenant . . . and I will remember the land."*
>
> (Leviticus 26:40, 42)

Summary

God has made a way for us to know His covering throughout our lives. This comes when we recognize and walk in His order for all our relationships and also in our own personal lives. God has ordained a rightful structure within marriage, families, communities and nations. This right structure establishes His direction, His protection and His nurture for each one of us. Those who are called to be shepherds carry a particular responsibility for maintaining God's cover over His people, but we are all called to be in right relationship with one another.

One of the pictures which may help us to understand God's covering, is to imagine a very strong umbrella giving shelter from a hail storm. Provided the umbrella is sound, the one holding it protects himself and all those walking with him, if they are moving in harmony with one another. Any of the group can choose to step away from the umbrella but the consequence is likely to be painful. The more we stay in line with God's order for our lives the more we will know the shelter which He longs to give us.

Many people describe their lives as having been spiritually unsafe, either at specific times of trauma or just in the everyday circumstances in which they found themselves. Sometimes this was because they had stepped away from the umbrella but often it was because the umbrella was full of holes due to the sinfulness of those carrying the responsibility of protection. We need to look next at what happens under an umbrella with holes.

CHAPTER 6

How we become exposed

Ignoring the warnings

How do we become exposed?

How does an umbrella become full of holes? Why do some people seem to experience so little godly protection in their lives? To understand the underlying reasons, we need to consider God's plan for protecting us – His laws and commands.

God wants every one of us to enjoy His blessing of covenant and covering. A covenant has terms and conditions, which state the boundaries under which the agreement applies. When we move outside these boundaries, we lose the right to claim the provisions and promises of the covenant. It is therefore very important that we firstly understand and recognize some foundational spiritual laws. Secondly, we need to follow God's commands, which are given in order that we can benefit from, rather than be harmed by, these spiritual laws.

The laws of physics can be beneficial or harmful to us depending on whether or not we respect those laws. If I ignore warning signposts and walk below an unstable rock face, I could well have a boulder land on my head, and the law of gravity would, in that moment, have done me rather more harm than good! It would be foolish to blame gravity. The truth is that this physical law is good for us only if we obey the rules.

It is just the same with God's spiritual laws. They were designed to be a blessing to us but if we go against God's commandments, which are His warning signs, we will find that those same laws will leave us exposed and likely to suffer harm. Throughout the Bible God has given many helpful commands to those who choose to listen. The benefit of following these commands has always been the opportunity to be in a covenant relationship with Him and to enjoy His shelter. God spelt it out to the Children of Israel, through ten specific commands which He gave to Moses:

> *"So He declared to you His covenant which He commanded you to perform, that is, the Ten Commandments; and He wrote them on two tablets of stone."*
>
> (Deuteronomy 4:13)

Throughout human history, people have mostly heeded warning signs which were intended for their physical safety, but have ignored God's signposts which were intended to give them spiritual protection.

Man found it impossible to obey even a few of God's commands, and would not listen to those people whom God sent to explain them. God's perfect plan was that Jesus would meet the terms and conditions of the covenant on our behalf. There is now a new simple command-ment which fulfills all the requirements of God's spiritual laws:

> *This is His commandment, that we believe in the name of His Son Jesus Christ, and love one another, just as He commanded us.*
>
> (1 John 3:23)

Jesus Himself made it very clear that His coming did not do away with God's spiritual laws but rather made a way for every one of us to benefit from them:

> *"Do not think that I came to abolish the Law or the Prophets; I did not come to abolish but to fulfill."*
>
> (Matthew 5:17)

This is how we benefit from God's laws: if we follow God's commandments, we enter His covenant with us. In covenant with God, there is a spiritual covering which gives direction, protection and nurture.

Umbrellas with holes

When we were young, we could not understand God's commands by ourselves, so God intended for us to be dependent on our parents and their own willingness to follow God's commands. If they were willing to walk with God, He provided a strong spiritual umbrella over the whole family which gave His protection against the spiritual hailstorms. The problem was that, if Dad was in fact breaking covenant with God through sin, the umbrella was not then intact. When an umbrella has holes in it, those underneath are exposed to the storm.

But as we saw in the last chapter, it is not just fathers who hold up God's spiritual umbrella over our lives. Our forebears, parents, teachers, community leaders, national leaders and of course we ourselves all participate in the godly order which brings God's shelter over our lives. Many of these people will have held up damaged umbrellas and some will have thrown the umbrella away completely!

One day Nehemiah looked at the condition of his own life, the people around him, and the damaged walls and gates of Jerusalem, and he saw clearly the history of broken covenant and the spiritual exposure which was now the consequence. He realized that it was time to agree with God's view of the situation.

> They said to me, "The remnant there in the province who survived the captivity are in great distress and reproach, and the wall of Jerusalem is broken down and its gates are burned with fire." When I heard these words, I sat down and wept and mourned for days; and I was fasting and praying before the God of heaven. I said, "I beseech You, O LORD God of heaven, the great and awesome God, who preserves the covenant and lovingkindness for those who love

> *Him and keep His commandments, let Your ear now be attentive*
> *and Your eyes open to hear the prayer of Your servant which I*
> *am praying before You now, day and night, on behalf of the sons*
> *of Israel Your servants, confessing the sins of the sons of Israel*
> *which we have sinned against You; I and my father's house have*
> *sinned."*
>
> (Nehemiah 1:3–6)

The condition of Jerusalem, with its broken walls, was a picture for Nehemiah of the spiritual exposure of the people, through the breaking of covenant with God, by himself and his forebears. God was using the honesty of Nehemiah's contrite heart to be the means by which He could re-cover His people. Nehemiah was being given the opportunity to hold up a new and intact umbrella over himself and those with him.

Damaged roofs allow the rot to set in

For complete protection against a storm, you need a house rather than just an umbrella. However, even with a strong dwelling, there is no quicker or more effective way to bring about the deterioration of a building than by ignoring a damaged roof. Umbrellas and roofs are both useful pictures for exploring this subject of protective covering. My wife and I lead the Ellel Ministries team based at Glyndley Manor. When Ellel took on the property some years ago, we had no idea that, even before the previous owners, there had been some serious roof damage by fire, with extremely poor repair work done.

Several years after the purchase of the property, wood rot was discovered in the conference room. A leaking roof creates damp conditions. The damp attracts fungal growth, destroying the wooden framework, which can then weaken the structure and let in more rain. This is an obvious but very accurate picture of how we can be affected by a damaged spiritual roof over our lives. When the godly covering is not intact, the exposure can give the enemy an opportunity to establish his conditions of spiritual darkness and distortion. Under these conditions, he can get a grip which perpetuates the very disorder which gave him access. We shall look later at the "fungal" activity of the powers of darkness.

Sometimes on our *Restoration Weeks* at Glyndley, we ask people to draw a simple picture of their lives, represented by a building. Many find themselves drawing distorted houses with poor foundations and incomplete roofs. One man said, "My childhood was like living life in a permanent storm, living in a home where the spiritual roof had blown away."

How does the protective roof over our lives get damaged?

Poor maintenance and storm damage

God provides the means of covering, but people are entrusted with the maintenance. We have been looking at all those to whom God has entrusted the maintenance of the covering for His people, including leaders, parents, forebears and, of course, ourselves. God has given to all these people the responsibility to maintain the spiritual roof over their own lives, and also over those for whom they carry a rightful responsibility. In reality the maintenance has very often been poor and the rain has found a way in, leading to damage in the fabric of people's lives.

When there has been neglect in keeping the roof of a building in a sound condition, the structure becomes very vulnerable to extreme storms. And so it has been for many children in families where God's order has been absent. The poor covering has left them exposed to life's traumas in ways which have had a significant and lasting impact on the spiritual, emotional and even physical well-being of their lives.

James was seven years old when he was suddenly moved with his parents from Singapore to the United States. Dad, who had always been very cold towards James, had taken a new job. Although the financial provision for the family was in place, the emotional and spiritual protection was very poor. Finding himself in a school playground surrounded by much bigger boys, who did not understand his Chinese language and ridiculed his small stature, James experienced a moment of total overwhelm. It was like being hit by a hurricane and the impact on his life was so much greater because of the serious lack of parental affirmation and nurture. The hurricane seemed to strip away the very fragile spiritual roof which had existed over his life.

As James described the incident to us, he realized that a part of him had become frozen in the trauma of the incident, gripped with fear and rejection. As we prayed, he saw for the first time how much he had hated himself in that moment because of his size and cultural background. As he confessed this, and forgave his parents and those at the school, we asked the Lord to restore His covering over this exposed part of James' life. Tears flowed and James experienced a powerful release from the enemy's grip, as he allowed Jesus to repair the roof and minister the acceptance and affirmation which he so needed. "I know it sounds silly," he said, "but I feel several inches taller and I am remembering, for the first time in twenty years, how to speak that Chinese dialect which I hated so much that day."

It is never too late to get right with God and to have the roof over our lives repaired!

Who left us uncovered?

God has made us to be dependent on Him, partly through our interdependence with one another. The sin of others can leave us exposed, particularly as small children, but this principle is relevant throughout our lives. Mercifully, God has the solution for exposure, however it is caused. We will explore this more later.

Whether we use the picture of an umbrella with holes, or a roof with the tiles missing, there is a reality of spiritual exposure in all of our lives. We have all been part of family groups, whether in a household, a community or a nation. In these families, apart from our own sin, there have been those who have broken covenant with God and left themselves and us spiritually exposed.

We can be uncovered through the sin of our forebears

Our fathers sinned, and are no more;
It is we who have borne their iniquities.

(Lamentations 5:7)

Remember, iniquity puts us out of line with God and exposed to the enemy. There is a striking pattern of disorder in some families: similar areas of sin and dysfunction seem to occur down a family line, not just through learned behavior but seemingly locked into the spiritual inheritance. The sin of our forebears puts a hole in the generational umbrella. Where particular sins have caused specific holes, the subsequent genera-tions are very often exposed and vulnerable in the same areas of sin.

We can be uncovered through the sin of our parents

From the start of our lives, the spiritual integrity of our parents gave us God's covering, whereas their sinfulness left us spiritually unpro-tected. Even the nature of our conception can affect our spiritual covering. It is worth noting that under the Old Testament law illegitimate children were prohibited from joining with God's people in worship: "No one of illegitimate birth shall enter the assembly of the Lord" (Deuteronomy 23:2). We have had the privilege of ministering to many people who have had a deep sense of exposure and isolation resulting from an illegitimate birth. God so wants each one of us to be confident that, in Christ, we truly belong to His family.

Through our lives we continue to be affected by the consequences of the sin of our parents. A father's trust in God (or lack of it) can have a very significant effect on the spiritual, emotional and physical well-being of his children. In the story of the boy with epilepsy, unbelief was a hole in the family umbrella:

*And He [Jesus] asked the father, "How long has this been happening
to him [your son]?" And he said, "From childhood. It has often
thrown him both into the fire and into the water to destroy him. But
if You can do anything, take pity on us and help us!" And Jesus said
to him, " 'If You can?' All things are possible to him who believes."
Immediately the boy's father cried out, "I do believe; help my
unbelief."*

(Mark 9:21–24)

Let me tell you briefly about Malcolm. He came for prayer, com-
plaining of headaches and physical problems which had resulted
from a lifetime of head injuries. We asked God what was going on.
He brought very clearly into Malcolm's memory the day that his
father had come home drunk and had beaten him violently about
the head. For a few moments, as we prayed, he experienced the
feelings of how it had been as a six-year-old and he acknowledged
that he had been fortunate not to be killed.

As he started to forgive his father, we realized that the trauma,
and the horrendous lack of a father's covering, had been like a
welcome notice to the enemy, in effect saying, "I give you a right
to harm this boy whenever you get an opportunity, especially with
head injury." As we sought the re-covering of God's spiritual
protection, we challenged the enemy's rights and addressed, among
others, a spirit of infirmity. There followed a remarkable restoration. Later we will explore more of how to pray into issues like
this.

We can be uncovered through the carelessness of the shepherds

One of the occasions when Malcolm again suffered head injury was
through the carelessness of a teacher at a particular school. The
pattern of spiritual exposure and injury had been started by dad,
but the enemy took full advantage of any subsequent opportunity.
As we realized this principle, we were able to pray for, and see, the
freedom and restoration which God desired.

Apart from parents, many other people have had responsibility for the well-being of our lives. They were like shepherds entrusted with sheep. When those people, rightly responsible for our care, abdicate that responsibility, the enemy can move in to devour. In the Old Testament, God appointed priests to be part of the shepherding of His people, the children of Israel. When they failed to provide that care, the people were exposed to all kinds of danger:

> *"As I live," declares the LORD God, "surely because My flock has become a prey, My flock has even become food for all the beasts of the field for lack of a shepherd, and My shepherds did not search for My flock, but rather the shepherds fed themselves and did not feed My flock . . . "*
>
> (Ezekiel 34:8)

Furthermore, they even brought spiritual exposure on the people through their own idolatry:

> *"Because they ministered to them before their idols and caused the house of Israel to fall into iniquity, therefore I have raised My hand in an oath against them," says the Lord GOD . . .*
>
> (Ezekiel 44:12 NKJV)

The sin of shepherds will very often lead a flock into iniquity and cause some to stumble and fall into similar sin.

We can be uncovered through the sin of those who have owned the ground which we occupy

> *Do not defile yourselves with any of these things; for by all these the nations are defiled, which I am casting out before you. For the land is defiled; therefore I visit the punishment of its iniquity upon it, and the land vomits out its inhabitants.*
>
> (Leviticus 18:24–25 NKJV)

Sin uncovers and defiles both people and the land. The spiritual distortion of iniquity clearly affects not just people but also their land and homes. Future occupants of that land can experience this spiritual hostility, unless they seek its cleansing through the forgiveness of those who sinned, and thereby receive God's restoration of fruitfulness.

Let me tell you about Jane. She came to Ellel Glyndley Manor asking for prayer for her neck. She had fallen down the stairs in her brother's house. She felt that God was telling her that this home, which had belonged to her parents, had always been a place of bitter contention and that she had been exposed to the spiritual defilement which existed there. She forgave those who had caused the defilement in the house and confessed her own part in the sinful relationships. We asked God to restore His covering and Jane experienced a wonderful healing.

We can be uncovered by bad government

When national leaders ignore God, whole nations can suffer the spiritual exposure. On countless occasions in the history of the nation of Israel, its leaders made decisions without first consulting God. These decisions always resulted in disaster for the nation, of which the following passage from Isaiah is just one example:

> *"Woe to the rebellious children," declares the* LORD,
> *"Who execute a plan, but not Mine,*
> *And make an alliance, but not of My Spirit,*
> *In order to add sin to sin;*
> *Who proceed down to Egypt*
> *Without consulting Me,*
> *To take refuge in the safety of Pharaoh*
> *And seek shelter in the shadow of Egypt!*
> *Therefore the safety of Pharaoh will be your shame*
> *And the shelter in the shadow of Egypt, your humiliation."*
>
> (Isaiah 30:1–3)

We live at a time now in history where, throughout the world, most people and nations reject the God of Israel, and see no reason to follow His instructions or to submit to the commands of His Son Jesus. Most of the world would regard it as ludicrous to consider God to be the only One who really knows what is right for mankind. Even some who accept the existence of God seem more convinced than ever of the effectiveness of man's own wisdom. Speaking about such people, Jesus said,

> " . . . in vain do they worship Me,
> teaching as doctrines the precepts of men."
>
> (Matthew 15:9)

But mankind sees that there is a big problem. The injustice and disorder in this world is evident to anyone who takes even a brief look. Well-meaning international leaders know that the condition of this world is not right. Whether through ignorance or pride, they don't see the possibility that the reason for the state of this world is the sin of every member of humanity. Instead of calling on the world community to behave towards one another in accordance with what God says is right, it has become a common theme over recent decades to declare that man has personal and inalienable rights to life, liberty and security. This sounds very plausible, but the Bible says that, without the forgiveness of God through Jesus Christ, we lose all these benefits, when we sin. If personal sin is ignored, no man-made declarations will ever get to the root problem.

We can all be uncovered by the sin of governments. When, for example, ungodly laws are passed in areas such as abortion and sexual behavior, every citizen becomes vulnerable to the enemy's destructive authority. I believe that the solution is to confront carefully with truth when appropriate, forgive the sins of those in government and pray that they will come to know God's ways. Our leaders (and consequently our nations) will benefit when we pray for them much more and criticize them much less.

We can be uncovered through the sin of spiritual brothers and sisters who should be covering our backs

Criticism, gossip and judgment between the members of a family leave each of them exposed. When relationships within the Body of Christ are contrary to God's command to love one another, the enemy again has opportunity to attack and even destroy. In Galatians 5:15 Paul writes:

> But if you bite and devour one another, take care that you are not consumed by one another.

What a difference there is when we cover one another with the protection of prayer rather than the slime of criticism. We can, on behalf of others, watch out for them and stand with God against the enemy. Those we intercede for will still be accountable for their own walk with the Lord, but our prayer can significantly disrupt the effectiveness of the enemy's battle plans.

Agreeing with God and following His instructions always has the effect of reducing the enemy's position of authority. This was clearly the case when Jesus sent out seventy-two of His disciples to go ahead of Him to the towns and villages, proclaiming the coming of the Kingdom of God. Luke recounts,

> The seventy returned with joy, saying, "Lord, even the demons are subject to us in Your name." And He [Jesus] said to them, "I was watching Satan fall from heaven like lightning."

> (Luke 10:17–18)

We can be uncovered through unexpected trauma

Sometimes things happen in life and they seem to come totally "out of the blue." Occasionally we can see (at least in part) why we were particularly vulnerable to an accident or trauma happening to us.

For example, we may have been driving when we were really too tired to concentrate. However, at other times things just seem to be the consequence of living in a fallen world where so many people are breaking covenant with God. Trauma often happens when we least expect it, as it did to the man in Jesus' parable of the Good Samaritan:

> *"A man was going down from Jerusalem to Jericho, and fell among robbers, and they stripped him and beat him, and went away leaving him half dead."*
>
> (Luke 10:30)

Life can sometimes overwhelm us so much that we feel broken or shattered by the experience. The Bible makes reference to this issue of brokenness in the heart and how vulnerable we can be when the integrity of our whole being has been shattered by traumatic events. A flock of sheep is very exposed when the shepherd does not provide protection from a hungry lion. The sheep become even more vulnerable when the flock is scattered. The prophet Ezekiel describes what happens when this scattering occurs:

> *"They were scattered for lack of a shepherd, and they became food for every beast of the field and were scattered."*
>
> (Ezekiel 34:5)

Brokenness within our own bodies can leave us similarly exposed. We will look further at this important principle later.

The traveler in the story of the Good Samaritan was apparently just going about his business, when he was suddenly attacked and stripped. Every trauma in our lives, whatever the cause, is a moment of potential spiritual exposure. This story goes on to explain how those with the heart of Jesus will seek to recover and to restore others from the places in their lives where they have been overwhelmed by painful events. We can be part of this.

Our own responsibility for God's covering

Simply put, our problem is that we have been wounded in life and
we have also sinned, and very often we have tried to cover the pain
or the shame by our own effort. Self-covering (self-protection) is a
big issue and we will look at that in more detail later. In the mean-
time we can sum it up by saying that when the human soul tries to
take charge over the human spirit, we are in trouble. Our spirit sees
and knows best under the anointing of the Holy Spirit, but we have
too often chosen to be wise in our own eyes. It can be a remarkable
place of healing to recognize this and come back under rightful
submission to the covering of the Spirit of God. Proverbs 3:7–8
says:

> *Do not be wise in your own eyes;*
> *Fear the* Lord *and turn away from evil.*
> *It will be healing to your body*
> *And refreshment to your bones.*

All sin leaves us exposed. For example, we can actively uncover
our lives through occult involvement, sexual immorality, drug abuse,
idolatry or wrong beliefs. When our soul follows our sinful nature
and ignores the wisdom of God, we leave ourselves uncovered and
very open to the enemy's deception.

> *This wisdom is not that which comes down from above, but is earthly,*
> *natural [soulish], demonic.*
>
> (James 3:15)

Because of the protection against the powers of darkness afforded
by God's covering, the enemy will certainly try to tempt us out from
this sheltered place. Satan tried it with Jesus, so there is no doubt that
he will try it with us. We noted in a previous chapter that Satan even
used a passage from Psalm 91, probably the most significant passage
on covering, to try to tempt Jesus out from His Father's protection.
Satan sought to persuade Jesus to call on angelic help. Angels were,

of course, poised to minister to Jesus at any time, but could only rightly operate within God's order, as Jesus followed His Father's instructions, rather than following the seduction of Satan.

Giving footholds to the enemy

When we are not under God's covering, there is an opportunity for the enemy to gain a place of spiritual authority in our lives. The only way that Satan and his domain of darkness have any ability to exercise authority in this world is when man acts independently of God's commands.

God's commands are given to human beings not to control them but to give them abundant life. When I am driving a car and I see a sign at a crossroads which commands me to stop, it would be foolish for me to be upset and say that it is controlling my life. I have a choice to disobey but it surely makes sense to heed the warning! God's commands in the Bible are also given to keep us out of trouble *and* out of the enemy's grip. For example, in Ephesians 4:26–27 the apostle Paul writes:

> *Be angry, and yet do not sin; do not let the sun go down on your anger, and do not give the devil an opportunity.*

Satan's basic desire is to gain spiritual authority through man's disobedience to God. As we saw earlier, he loses authority through our obedience. Recording the effect on Satan's place of authority as the disciples followed the Lord's instructions to preach, heal and deliver those in spiritual captivity, Jesus said, "I was watching Satan fall from heaven like lightning" (Luke 10:18).

It is through sin that man destroys God's covering. Satan then takes advantage of this opportunity to assume his own spiritual authority in our lives, to promote his destructive purposes. He began this process in the Garden of Eden as man first followed an instruction from the serpent, in rebellion to God. Satan continued with the upper hand in every generation until one day a man called Jesus, walking in the wilderness, said "No" to every tempting suggestion

of the enemy. Jesus has been given, and has retained, *all* authority
and we enter into the most secure place in the universe when we
belong to Him.

Wrong covenants

Because of the foundational significance of covenant in our relationship with God and the spiritual covering which follows, Satan seeks
particularly to draw individuals, families and nations into wrong
covenants. These give a particularly strong opportunity for the powers
of darkness to exert control and a false covering over those involved.
This can be either through their personal involvement or through
the sins of those holding the spiritual umbrella. In the history of the
people of Israel, Joshua and his fellow leaders made a wrong covenant
on behalf of God's people, with disastrous results:

> *So the men of Israel took some of their [the Gibeonites'] provisions,*
> *and did not ask for the counsel of the LORD. Joshua made peace with*
> *them and made a covenant with them, to let them live; and the leaders*
> *of the congregation swore an oath to them.*
>
> (Joshua 9:14–15)

They had in fact been deceived by a neighboring nation that God
had commanded them to destroy, which left them exposed to a
damaging enemy foothold in the land.

A wrong covenant is an ungodly alliance, usually with people but
indirectly with the spiritual realm of darkness, through a combina-
tion of vows, rituals and oaths. Whether or not the participants are
aware of the spiritual significance, it is a very exposed place.

> *Because you have said, "We have made a covenant with death,*
> *And with Sheol we have made a pact . . .*
> *For we have made falsehood our refuge and we have concealed*
> *ourselves with deception."*
> *. . . I [God] will make justice the measuring line and righteousness*
> *the level;*

Then hail will sweep away the refuge of lies
And the waters will overflow the secret place.

(Isaiah 28:15, 17)

Sometimes in occult practices, covenants are made directly with the powers of darkness. I remember talking to Jean, who confessed that she had allowed a man practicing witchcraft to carry out a ritual, involving animal sacrifice, on her behalf. It was, in effect, a pact with the enemy to give her special powers in business and over the men in her life. She indeed found herself exercising remarkable supernatural abilities, but the false covenant had brought devastating damage to her health and life, until that day when Jesus broke her free from the ungodly alliance.

Looking at Freemasonry sometimes provides a useful example of the enemy's strategies. It is a fellowship of men based on powerful and destructive practices. The vows and oaths spoken by candidates, together with the rituals enacted, are clear statements of covenant, but not with the true God. It can seem very attractive to dwell in fellowship with a group of men who promise to cover each other's backs in difficult situations, but it is a place of false security.

The godly roof over families is severely damaged by husbands and fathers entering into these ungodly alliances and the enemy can gain a significant foothold in the family line. Praise God that He has made a way of resolving this, by establishing a true dwelling for our safety.

Therefore thus says the Lord GOD,
"Behold I am laying in Zion a stone, a tested stone,
A costly cornerstone for the foundation, firmly placed.
He who believes in it will not be disturbed."

(Isaiah 28:16)

The story of Naomi

The Bible has many wonderful stories of God's covering lost and redeemed. Let's look again at the book of Ruth, from the viewpoint of Naomi. We see a father putting his whole family into a place of serious spiritual exposure. The man's name is Elimelech and his wife is Naomi. There is famine in his home town of Bethlehem and instead of seeking God in this rightful place of God's people, he moves the whole family away and into enemy territory, the land of Moab. It is here that the problems really start: Elimelech dies and his sons marry Moabite women, Ruth and Orpah.

After some time the sons also die, and Naomi is left without the protection of her husband or her sons. She is apparently completely uncovered, but she clearly believes in a redeeming God and she hears of the provision of food back in Judah. Together with Ruth, she returns home in simple dependence on her God and she discovers His faithfulness as He restores her into His covering through the marriage of Ruth to Boaz. As Ruth gives birth to a son, it is clear to all those around Naomi that God has amazingly restored her into the protective family of His choice:

> *Then the women said to Naomi, "Blessed is the LORD who has not left you without a redeemer today, and may his name become famous in Israel. May he also be to you a restorer of life and a sustainer of your old age; for your daughter-in-law, who loves you and is better to you than seven sons, has given birth to him."*

(Ruth 4:14–15)

Whatever the experiences of our lives, God has promised, by His covenant, to be a Father to His children when we trust in Him. His ways are not our ways but His promise to cover us will never be broken.

God sees and restores uncovered lives

There is another amazing story in the Bible of a young man who certainly experienced a life which was constantly being exposed by the sin of others. Remarkably, he manages to keep his heart right with God and discovers that He has been preparing to use him to be His means of provision and protection for all His people, even through the sinfulness of others. The one who was so poorly covered by others, eventually becomes the one whom God uses to cover a nation. The young man's name was Joseph.

Let me remind you of Joseph's story:

Joseph was uncovered through the sins of deception and favoritism in his family line, particularly on the part of his father. Jacob himself had deceived his own father and he seemed unable to deal fairly and honestly with his sons. Joseph was given wrong clothing, wrong advice regarding his dreams and wrong instructions regarding his brothers (Genesis 37:3–11).

He was uncovered through the jealousy and deception of his older brothers, stripped and abandoned (Genesis 37:18–34).

He was uncovered by the lust and abuse of the mistress of the Egyptian household, where he had become a respected slave (Genesis 39:1–18).

He was uncovered by the lack of protection by the master of the same household, who permitted false accusation to stand unchallenged (Genesis 39:19–20).

He was uncovered by the carelessness of a fellow prisoner in jail, who forgot, at least initially, to speak up for Joseph (Genesis 40:9–23).

Through all of his trials, Joseph managed to walk with a right heart towards God. He was eventually, after thirteen long years, recovered to a place of dignity and authority through the needs, wisdom and instructions of Pharaoh. Under the direction of Pharaoh, Joseph was restored into a place of order and personal covering (Genesis 41:14–44).

Step by step, Joseph chose to face the abuse and pain of the past and was reconciled with his brothers (Genesis 45:1–4).

In this place of personal recovery, Joseph became God's means of covering for whole nations, to protect them from the destruction of the famine (Genesis 45:5–9).

After reading this story, who can doubt that we have a God who re-covers and restores lives, in order that each one of us can fully enter the personal destiny which He has prepared? We have all been exposed by our own sin and the sin of others in our past. As we bring these situations with a right heart before God, He will embrace our lives again in His protective arms. It is not a dream. It is the truth of a covenant-keeping Father who loves us.

A summary

God has established spiritual and physical laws. They are for our benefit provided that we obey His instructions. When we do follow His commands, we enter a covenant relationship with Him in which He promises to provide for us and protect us.

His commands require us to live in ordered relationships with one another respecting the principles which He has ordained including family, marriage, parenting and leadership. Within these relationship groups God's spiritual covering is established, just like a strong umbrella being held over a family by a caring dad.

Disobeying God's law and His order breaks covenant with Him, and the spiritual umbrellas become damaged. Everyone sheltering under the umbrella is affected by the holes, and the exposure gives opportunity for the enemy to bring disorder into the lives of all those involved.

Since the Fall, man has always been painfully aware of the feelings of being uncovered, whether he admits to it or not. In his desire to find spiritual shelter, he has consistently tried to solve the problem by his own effort. We now need to look at the ineffectiveness of self-protection and self-covering.

CHAPTER 7

The deception of self-covering

*Believing that we can provide our
own spiritual protection*

Living inside our own shell

There is something very appealing about being able to have a strong portable dwelling into which we could disappear at any time of the day. It almost seems unfair that the tortoise has this opportunity. As soon as he feels exposed, he can withdraw into the safety of his shell. It's the perfect self-protection, but I guess there have to be some benefits to being a tortoise!

Some of us also try to construct our own shell. Instead of finding the strong spiritual dwelling place which God offers through Jesus, we prefer to provide our own. Unfortunately it is a shelter of fantasy. Proverbs 18:10–11 says:

> *The name of the LORD is a strong tower;*
> *The righteous runs into it and is safe.*
> *A rich man's wealth is his strong city,*
> *And like a high wall in his own imagination.*

For all sorts of reasons we seek to cover wounds and pain, as well as sin. It is difficult to be honest about all the hurts inside, particularly for men, it seems. There is a fear of a negative response from people, a fear of rejection, a fear of experiencing further pain and a fear of people finding out what we are *really* like!

Those in government hate to be found out when mistakes have been made, and the newspapers often proclaim their cover-up actions as a *whitewash*. Hiding what is dark by using white paint, literally or figuratively, has always, it seems, been an attractive option. The prophet Ezekiel complained:

> *"It is definitely because they have misled My people by saying, 'Peace!' when there is no peace. And when anyone builds a wall, behold, they plaster it over with whitewash."*
>
> (Ezekiel 13:10)

Jesus gets a bit more personal with the scribes and Pharisees. They are presenting themselves as being right with God, but it's a cover-up.

> *"Woe to you, scribes and Pharisees, hypocrites! For you are like white-washed tombs which on the outside appear beautiful, but inside they are full of dead men's bones and all uncleanness."*
>
> (Matthew 23:27)

There is a powerful challenge for us all here. What dark or dead places have I covered over on the inside, in order to appear OK on the surface?

We do have a choice about how we seek to restore spiritual protection to the exposed places in our lives, but we need to use that choice wisely. What seems to us a convenient way of protection, can end up destroying the very person who God has made us to be. It is like deciding to tear apart a city, to get materials to build up the boundary walls, instead of seeking wise counsel about how to defend the inhabitants, which is something the prophet Isaiah accused the leaders of Israel of doing when the city was facing attack:

> *And you saw that the breaches*
> *In the wall of the city of David were many;*

And you collected the waters of the lower pool.
Then you counted the houses of Jerusalem
And tore down houses to fortify the wall.
And you made a reservoir between the two walls
For the waters of the old pool.
But you did not depend on Him who made it,
Nor did you take into consideration Him who planned it long ago.

(Isaiah 22:9–11)

Not just any covering, but His cover!

We have been reminded that in the Garden of Eden God formed man through the fusion of created dust and His breath of life. Only mankind is made in the image of God, who is Spirit: we are physical beings with a spirit given by Him. This amazing joining of the physical and spiritual realms is unique in man. As Genesis 1:24 makes clear, animals are not made in the image of God, but only after their own kind: "Then God said, "Let the earth bring forth living creatures after their kind . . . "

Because we are both physical and spiritual beings, we need both physical and spiritual protection if we are to grow and flourish. God designed us to live in a perfect state of well-being, under His covering. His Spirit was meant to cover and direct our human spirit. When we are in this relationship with God, we are free to safely enjoy the extraordinary environment of the created world into which He has placed us and given us dominion.

Because true relationship depends on the freedom to choose, God not only gave clear instructions how to stay under His cover, but He also entrusted us with the ability to agree or disagree with His commands. The human soul (the interface of the human body and the human spirit) is designed to register both physical and spiritual information and to make the choices that progress us through life. When Adam and Eve chose to be directed by a created and fallen spiritual being, called Satan, rather than by the Spirit of God, they denied the Lord's light and direction in their human spirit and put themselves in a place of darkness and serious exposure, physically as well as spiritually.

No longer covered by their true spiritual Father, they were afraid, ashamed and desperate. Then they did something that mankind has continued to do ever since that moment. They tried to cover themselves, thinking *anything is better than nothing*. How wrong they were! Since the Fall, it has been our natural instinct to pursue a "cover-up." Caught by a teacher in the act of wrongdoing, it is common for schoolchildren to deal with the exposure by telling lies. Being led by our sinful nature, we have become experts at self-protection.

Fig leaves are cheap, but you get what you pay for

On the face of it, covering the problem may not seem to us a wrong thing to do. Adam and Eve thought it a good plan to sew leaves together and cover their bodies and the sense of vulnerability which they were feeling. The trouble was that they were designed to know true safety only under God's covering. Any self-sufficient attempt to meet this deep spiritual need was only going to end in more distress. Try giving an astronaut an anorak for protection as he walks on the moon. The idea is as crazy as expecting fig leaves to protect us from spiritual exposure!

Right here, God started a journey of recovery with mankind by giving Adam and Eve a covering of skins. God's first lesson was that *He* must be the Provider and that it was going to be very costly, even requiring the shedding of blood. When we receive God's true covering it restores the spiritual well-being of our lives. When we resort to self-covering it only brings further separation between us and our Heavenly Father. This has been a foundational cause of dysfunction in mankind as human beings have striven, in pride and ignorance, to find ways of feeling more secure in the place of the exposure which sin creates.

Covering ourselves comes naturally

Of course, sewing leaves together is a less common way of getting covered up these days, but we are still very motivated by appearances. After a Sunday church service, when a friend asks us how we are, many of us will quickly say, "Oh fine!"

For most of the congregation it's not true. It's a cover-up!

In many societies, it is very important to be seen to be self-composed and having no real problems. If we *do* have problems, we like to think that we can sort it out ourselves! We don't just feel the need to pretend to others but we even pretend to ourselves as well! When our words or the expression on our face do not match the condition of our hearts, there is a covering of unreality in place. We can dress with style and exude confidence through our tailored suit or fashionable clothes but it may well be covering over a helpless sense of inadequacy, guilt or pain.

The vicar's collar and robes may mark him out as having a priestly role, but if his evenings are spent viewing pornography on the Internet, God is unimpressed by the garments in which he has clothed himself. Self-covering can be a form of self-righteousness. Both leave us very vulnerable to the enemy's accusation and sifting. As Jesus' death was approaching, He warned His disciple Peter of a time of testing that lay ahead of him: "Simon, Simon, behold Satan has demanded permission to sift you like wheat . . . " (Luke 22:31). Peter's response to Jesus' words was gross unreality: "Lord, with You I am ready to go both to prison and to death!" (Luke 22:33). It covered deep fears which he had not yet been willing to face. Sooner or later our lives get shaken and sifted, so that the unseen wounds and sins rise to the surface.

As we go about our lives, if we are really honest with ourselves, we very often know that we feel exposed somewhere inside, but we try self-help, self-sufficiency, self-improvement and self-protection. Unfortunately, all these practices are independent of the only One who really *does* have the solution, but somehow we feel so sure that we know best.

David had a big fight on his hands one day. The opposition was called Goliath. Following Saul's advice, David tried the heavy man-made armor and weapons, but he soon realized that it could only be God's protection that would bring him victory over the enemy:

> *Then David said to the Philistine, "You come to me with a sword, a spear, and a javelin, but I come to you in the name of the* LORD *of hosts, the God of the armies of Israel, whom you have taunted."*
>
> (1 Samuel 17:45)

It was a good lesson for the future for David to trust only in God's covering.

Passive and aggressive self-covering

We cover up the hurting parts of our lives and erect a warning notice to the world around us, and even to ourselves, which says, "Don't go there!" The way we protect ourselves can be both passive and active; by that I mean we can either withdraw into hiding or we can make getting near very unpleasant for those around us. We can be a tortoise or a porcupine. The wounding that causes us to self-protect may well have been the result of the sin of others, but our ungodly defensive behaviors are sin of our own making.

Prickly, angry, arrogant people are very often covering up the pain of places of rejection and insecurity. People say that attack is the best form of defense, but they have forgotten the protection of the One who made them. As the psalmist recognized, critical, judgmental attitudes may seem to stop others hurting us first, but inside this defensive perimeter we become defiled, reaping the consequence of our sinful behaviors:

> *But he clothed himself with cursing as with his garment,*
> *And it entered into his body like water*
> *And like oil into his bones.*
>
> (Psalm 109:18)

Our responses may not necessarily be harmful to others but our self-built walls destroy true relationship. Many people have learned the art of laughing off every painful issue in their lives. The laughter is an inappropriate defense, hiding the real emotions and it eventually becomes uncomfortable for all those around. On the other hand, many Christians have become joyless and lifeless as a result of disconnection with the reality and the feelings of past events. Significant parts of their lives have been suppressed and left behind in a permanent shell which covers the pain.

It is not just wounding that we try to cover. The guilt of our own sin is painful to face and demands to be covered up. You see lots of people in the media today who have become experts at hiding guilt with either lies or the arrogance of a self-righteous morality. We find their views helpful in dealing with our own guilty feelings. It can be very comforting to hear someone else declare that our sin is not *really* sin. Sexual promiscuity can't *really* be sin if everyone is involved . . . can it? Why do people get caught up in the horrors of genocide, joining in with the atrocities? If enough people say that a behavior is OK, then we can become blinded to the truth.

It is a corporate cover up!

In the story by Hans Christian Andersen entitled *The Emperor's New Clothes*, it was not until a small child shouted out that the king was actually naked, that everybody could dare to face the truth of the deception. The king was supposed to be wearing a garment of the finest material but it was just not true. Christians today need to be confidently and clearly declaring what God says and not what the world says.

Self-covering starts early in life

For a young child, it is not primarily their own sin which leaves them exposed but the sin of those whom God has put in place to be the means of His protection, the ones holding the umbrella.

Little children start their lives very open to the world around them both physically and spiritually. God designed them to interact with their environment in a very simple and vulnerable way, guarded not by themselves but by the care of loving parents. For many children it is not long before they experience the sin and hostility in the world, often through unsafe parenting. From within their own fallen nature the child looks for ways to begin to find protection. Tiny babies have little ability to make rational assessments with their minds, but they are very aware of the spiritual environment which surrounds them. When the atmosphere is hostile, self-defense is a natural response.

Amazingly, such awareness can even start in the womb. We have prayed for many Christians who have acknowledged their day-to-day struggle to embrace life. Fears and uncertainties seem to constantly rise up within them restricting their ability to enter fully into the abundant life which Jesus has promised. On occasions while receiving prayer, the Lord has made some people aware that, because of an unsafe home environment when they were in the womb, there became established deep in their heart a resistance to being born. Through confession and forgiveness, God can re-establish His spiritual cover over any moment of our lives and restore to us His life-giving protection. For many who bring these kind of issues before the Lord, and make a fresh proclamation to *choose life*, we have witnessed a remarkable change as God restores the spiritual safety which had been stolen for so long.

Experts at hiding the truth

As we grow up, we become ever more aware of how unsafe life can be. Penny came to one of our centers asking for help. She had been emotionally and physically abused as a little girl, but whenever she talked about what had happened, she felt no emotion whatsoever. In fact she lived her life without true feelings and it was destroying relationships with those around her. We talked with Penny and asked the Lord to help us understand the truth of what was happening. We asked her how, at the time, she had dealt with the horrible things which had been done and said to her. "Well, I certainly didn't cry," she said, "that would just have got me into even more trouble. So I learnt to swallow hard and just get on with my life."

We realized God was showing us that the seemingly insignificant action of swallowing down the feelings had become Penny's little ritual for covering pain when situations became overwhelming. It was amazing, as she recognized and confessed the behavior, how

God released her from the spiritual hold of this understandable, but ungodly, covering technique. For the first time in nearly twenty years she was able to express true feelings and allow God to wrap His loving arms of comfort around her. Penny needed to learn to walk in this new lifestyle, but God had set her on an exciting new journey.

When events in our lives seem too hard to face, we sometimes choose to disconnect from the reality of how it really feels. It is a way of covering the pain, but the wound just remains unhealed in the disconnected place. This kind of dissociation from reality is like closing the door to a room in our house in order to shut away a distressing scene. Think what would happen if we actually did close off a room in our home, where, say, our pet cat had died. The problem would not go away and would certainly become very evident sooner or later!

Many of us have learned similar ways of doing this in our minds. When we make a choice to dissociate from a part of our past, even unconsciously, we are actually just hiding that place under fig leaves. Not having to face the problem may seem to help us, but it never brings lasting peace.

Disconnecting with the deep traumas of life

It can be hard for us to acknowledge that we have disconnected or broken away from a part of ourselves that has experienced physical and emotional pain. The problem is that, when we choose to leave a broken part of ourselves behind, we are working against God's desire for our wholeness. We can dissociate from our past in various ways, from just being unwilling to face an issue to literally breaking all emotional ties with a hurting part of life. People occasionally even experience an extreme type of separation which allows them, in the moment of trauma, to be observing themselves like a spectator. Brokenness, or loss of wholeness, is out of God's order. Disconnecting is another way of our covering the hurting places, places to which God wants to bring light, protection and restoration.

At times, events can even be so overwhelming that it seems that our soul and spirit can be fractured by the experience. We sometimes hear people say that they were "shattered" by a traumatic event, or that they just "went to pieces." It is not a choice consciously made but a reaction to the physical and emotional overwhelm. It is like an automatic trip switch responding to an electrical overload. Our emotional and spiritual circuits can get broken. Proverbs 15:13 says:

A joyful heart makes a cheerful face,
But when the heart is sad, the spirit is broken.

We will look more at this in another chapter.

The reality of these coping mechanisms may be an uncomfortable fact in many of our lives, but it is such an important principle to understand for our healing. Sometimes we need to be reminded that God really does know every detail and every moment of our existence. If any part of us could remain completely hidden from God, what an opportunity the enemy would have to rule there without a challenge. As it is, God longs to bring all the places known to Him, but may be hidden to us, into the light. He wants us to abandon our self-covering and receive His covering, wholeness and freedom to the broken and imprisoned parts of our identity.

The ways we try to escape

We look for escape from painful reality in many different ways. Trying to cover up anxiety in the heart leads people into count-less unhelpful activities. Self-denial, bravado, making a joke of it, running away, obsessive work, extreme exercise, food, alcohol and recreational drugs can all seem to provide a solution for hiding the pain, but they never resolve the issue.

Let me tell you Bill's story. He was overweight and seeking God's help in tackling his eating habits, which had started as a teenager, when he was ridiculed for his Jewish background. As we prayed, he began to realize that putting on weight had been an unconscious way of hiding himself, attempting to conceal the person on the inside whom he could not change. It wasn't rational but Bill knew that this had been his way of trying to cover his vulnerable identity. It was wonderful to see him renouncing this lifelong behavior, asking God to be his new protection and finding a new place of freedom.

Some of our covering techniques can be particularly harmful. Hallucinatory drugs (including strong forms of cannabis) break down the integrity of the body, soul and spirit relationship. When people say they have been on a "trip," using drugs, they are referring to an out-of-body experience which puts them, spiritually, in a very exposed place. We are meant to operate in godly wholeness and order, not spread about like the scattered contents of a broken suitcase. When such items are returned to the case, they will bring back all the dirt of the ground on which they fell. Drug-induced trips will invariably bring back demons. The mental and physical effects can appear years after the actual drug use.

Regarding prescribed drugs, there are, of course, many occasions when these are very helpful to alleviate symptoms. As we seek God for the fullness of His healing, it is always wise to ask Him to cover the effects of all medication, especially where it interferes with our normal consciousness. We want to receive all the benefits of the medicine and let God protect us from anything that would harm us.

Not facing the issue doesn't make it go away

Christine had a violent outburst of jealous anger against her husband the week before she came on an Ellel Ministries course teaching about emotional damage. She realized that there was an unhealed place in her life. It related to a day, thirty years before, when her then fiancé had told her that he had been seeing someone else, that this other person was pregnant, and that the engagement was off.

The news had caused Christine's world to fall completely apart. She had subsequently suffered years of depression and isolation. As she shared the story with us she realized that she had made a decision at the time to cover up all the pain, anger, jealousy and rejection by walking away and, in effect, leaving that episode in the cellar of her life, firmly hidden behind a trap door.

The event had certainly crushed her spirit but she had made a choice, contrary to God's order, to hide this part of herself in the basement. As if to make the point, she moved away from the district and away from all the friends she had known. It seemed the best way at the time of dealing with the overwhelming feelings. As we prayed, she chose to open the trap door and let Jesus go with her down into the painful events. She chose no longer to walk away from the truth of what had happened but to walk through the distress. This allowed the crushed part of her to come out of the darkness and into a new place of reality and wholeness. It was wonderful to see God bring powerful healing and deliverance.

Many of us have hidden a part of ourselves behind a trap door, to which the enemy now has the right of access, keeping a part of us separated from abundant life. The godly order of our bodies has been distorted by this decision, which may have seemed the only option at the time. Our minds and our wills acted in self-defense, with the consequence that our human spirit has not been fully free to follow the directions of God. The Lord wants us to choose to let Him restore His order and to walk again by the Spirit. In Romans 8:6 Paul writes,

> For the mind set on the flesh is death, but the mind set on the Spirit is life and peace . . .

We are made to live with the soul in rightful submission to the human spirit, which in turn is directed by the Spirit of God. In this way we can walk safely in God's order and under His covering.

Virtual worlds

Fantasy can offer a tempting way of covering painful reality. It is an attractive prospect to enter another world where my problems do not exist. There is nothing wrong with enjoying the respite of a

good novel for a while, but if our desire is to avoid reality, beware!
Jesus has strong words for the religious leaders who have given
authority to the enemy through their unreality:

> *"You are of your father, the devil . . . Whenever he speaks a lie, he*
> *speaks from his own nature, for he is a liar and the father of lies."*
>
> (John 8:44)

So many people are trying to kid others and even themselves that
all is well, when actually they are living in darkness.

Interestingly it is now becoming an option, in these days of the
Internet revolution, to enter virtual worlds where we can choose
our identity, our past, our present and our future. We can participate
in a world of virtual relationships and activities which avoid painful
reality and we can be the person we choose to be, rather than the
person we truly are. These possibilities can move quickly from enter-
tainment to dangerous fantasy, particularly when we look to these
escape routes to meet emotional or sexual needs. Satan inhabits the
world of fantasy when it is used to avoid truth.

Spies are often given a false identity and a false past, in order to
protect them in the dangerous world of espionage. This identity is
called their *cover*. Whether the practice of spying is right or wrong,
the most dangerous time for them is when their cover is blown.
Living in a fantasy world is a very unsafe existence. When we are
living in the truth there is no risk of sudden exposure.

False religion – the corporate search for spiritual cover

Since the start of human history, the need for spiritual cover has
been evident to every tribe, race and culture. Each human being
has known the fear of being exposed to spiritual lawlessness. Many
have sought to appease the spiritual beings of the unseen realm
by following religious practice which is intended to give some
measure of protection and provision along the journey of life.
Unfortunately, the Bible clearly explains that all religious practice

which does not acknowledge Jesus is a false spiritual covering. When we seek to appease the spiritual realm without following the truth of Jesus, we just give the enemy more authority to empower those religious practices. This promotes Satan's character in this fallen world.

The enemy is very willing to adopt any disguise which fools man into believing that he has found light in the discomfort of spiritual darkness. In 2 Corinthians 11:14 Paul tells us that he can even disguise himself as an "angel of light." Enlightenment has been man's quest for countless generations. However, all religious practice without Jesus is a man-made, enemy-empowered, false and destructive light. Such "light" is described in these verses:

> *Who is among you that fears the LORD,*
> *That obeys the voice of His servant,*
> *That walks in darkness and has no light?*
> *Let him trust in the name of the LORD and rely on his God.*
> *Behold, all you who kindle a fire,*
> *Who encircle yourselves with firebrands,*
> *Walk in the light of your fire*
> *And among the brands you have set ablaze.*
> *This you will have from My hand:*
> *You will lie down in torment.*

(Isaiah 50:10–11)

It is very hard to see the stars through the artificial lighting of a city. Again religious practice like Freemasonry gives a good example. It purports to offer ordinary decent men fellowship and enlightenment, but it is amazing how it blinds them to the true light of Christ. Really getting right with God is very different from following the rituals of appeasement required by much religious activity. In the story of Cain and Abel, we find that an offering of the harvest of the ground is inadequate. Only through the shedding of blood, it seems, can God's covering be restored. In fact, even this sacrifice would eventually need to be provided by God Himself.

God will not heal masks!

God has designed us to be dependent on His provision. When we ignore this and try to fend for ourselves, the result is doubly damaging. We lose God's best and actually resist His restoration, by establishing our own solution. The prophet Jeremiah uses a vivid image to describe this very human tendency:

> *"For My people have committed two evils:*
> *They have forsaken Me,*
> *The fountain of living waters,*
> *To hew for themselves cisterns,*
> *Broken cisterns*
> *That can hold no water."*
>
> (Jeremiah 2:13)

Some while ago, just before we were about to start a training school at Ellel Glyndley Manor, I remember being stopped in the kitchen by a member of the team. She had been praying about the delegates who would soon be arriving for a few weeks of teaching about the healing ministry of Jesus. She felt it important to pass on to me what God had been saying to her. "I believe that God wants to remind us," she said, "that He will not heal what He has not created."

As the School progressed I found myself pondering these words and they began to make more and more sense. It became apparent that there were a number of delegates who had been very wounded in their early lives. In order to protect the places of hurt they had unconsciously developed personalities which they presented to the world around them, in the expectation that this would make them more acceptable. But this mask was not the God-created person whom God truly wanted to heal; it was in fact a cover-up! They had not intended to create this false personality, but it had just grown through years of self-protection.

When we had opportunity to minister to the delegates during the prayer times, the Spirit of God brought conviction to them of the layers which had covered the real person inside. We have many times found that, as we seek healing for those who have been wounded by poor spiritual covering in their lives, it has frequently involved recognizing the self-covering which God wants removed rather than healed! Our choice to take away our defenses can feel very vulnerable, but we are letting God bring His true covering to the person He really loves underneath. It is true that God has no interest in restoring what is not part of His own creation.

Self-protection is a refuge of lies

We can wrongly believe that, if we pretend to be someone who fits the expectations of those around us, it will alleviate our insecurity and bring peace. But the very opposite is true. By negating the reality of who we really are and presenting an unreal face, we create division in the very core of our being. Our true identity is sealed within our human spirit. When we deny who God made us to be, we embrace deception and crush our own hearts.

I had a personal experience of God revealing to me how I had done this cover-up within myself for much of my life. My whole body reflected the stress of the division which had happened within me. Of course, I had not sat down as a little boy and consciously decided to hide part of the real me. It was just something that grew as I responded to a world which seemed to demand good children, good exam results, successful young men and happy families. I realized, through the conviction of the Holy Spirit, that I had developed a life-long skill in only presenting the acceptable part of me, but it was covering up a part that was imperfect, insecure and very anxious. I did not set out to deceive anyone but it had always seemed the only way to cope with life.

I realized that the unconscious cover-up of the real me, which was wounded and sinful, did not bring peace but, on the contrary, simply buried a fearful and distressed part of me on the inside. One way or another that wounded part makes itself known through emotional and physical dysfunction and sin, and that became my experience. Whether we intend it or not, self-protection leads to unreality, when we try to present to the world a person who is different from the one God created. In the words of Isaiah 28:15b, "we have made falsehood our refuge and we have concealed ourselves with deception."

God has a simple but powerful solution. If we respond to Him, Jesus will provide a truthful and unshakable place of protection for the person who God made us to be. Then the refuge of lies will be swept away.

> *Therefore thus says the Lord* GOD,
> *"Behold, I am laying in Zion a stone, a tested stone,*
> *A costly cornerstone for the foundation, firmly placed.*
> *He who believes in it will not be disturbed.*
> *I will make justice the measuring line*
> *And righteousness the level;*
> *Then hail will sweep away the refuge of lies*
> *And the waters will overflow the secret place."*
>
> (Isaiah 28:16–17)

God's covering is a dwelling place of truth

It is God's heart to bring all of us into a deeper place of His covering and restoration, if we are willing to respond to His direction. The man-made cover-ups need to be swept away through confession and repentance. We need to agree with God about the hurt and sin. There also needs to be forgiveness of those who have left us without godly covering and caused us to feel that we needed to fend for ourselves.

God's way of covering relies on absolute truth, and this can at first seem too transparent, too vulnerable, too exposing. What if everyone sees what we are really like? However, the fact is that when God is allowed to restore His right covering, the fears really do get replaced by His love.

I can give personal testimony to the fact that it works! When we face the truth, give up the self-protection and let God cover and restore the anxious places, there can be a radical change to the whole of our well-being. God wants us to be a people who will literally dwell in truth and holiness. Through the prophet Zechariah He promises:

> *"Thus says the* LORD, *'I will return to Zion and will dwell in the midst of Jerusalem. Then Jerusalem will be called the City of Truth, and the mountain of the* LORD *of hosts will be called the Holy Mountain.' "*
>
> (Zechariah 8:3)

A summary

We know that we need spiritual covering. In the absence of a covenant relationship with God, man has pursued his own protection, individually and corporately, ever since the Fall in the Garden of Eden.

Whether through self-reliance, man-made religion or putting on a mask, we attempt to provide the safety that our heart longs to experience. We can even choose, consciously or unconsciously, to hide the wounded or sinful parts of our lives by emotionally disconnecting from these painful places. It all amounts to a cover-up and to living a lie.

Facing the reality of this and letting God be the protector of every part of our lives can bring radical healing to body, soul and spirit. Before we explore more of this wonderful truth of God's healing, we need to take a serious look at the damage caused by spiritual exposure. A doctor usually knows what disorder he needs to treat by carefully investigating the symptoms. Checking the bad fruit in our lives can point to the root problem.

CHAPTER 8

The consequence of exposure

How has it affected me?

What happens when we are uncovered?

Sometimes we can remember the events in our lives when spiritual hailstorms battered us and caused damage. However, sometimes the memory of these times has been lost, maybe through choice or maybe because it was all so overwhelming. Either way, often we are still carrying today the consequence of past spiritual exposure.

Jenny was on a weekend course looking at the topic of inner healing. She knew that she had a problem but didn't understand the root. Anxiety, anger and shame sometimes rose up at unexpected moments and the intensity of these feelings had, over the years, caused considerable distress to both her and her husband. She knew it was associated with a self-rejection of her femininity and her physical appearance.

As Jenny listened to the teaching, God reminded her of an incident at the age of thirteen. She had been on holiday with her parents and late at night had gone from her bedroom to go to the bathroom, when she met her father on his way to bed. Jenny lowered her head as she described what happened next. Quite unexpectedly her father had lifted her nightdress and had casually said, "Well, let me see how my daughter is growing into a young woman." He had said nothing more and had quickly walked on.

She didn't know what had caused her father to behave in that way. It was out of character, but Jenny was overwhelmed with confused feelings as she recalled the moment. It had only been a few seconds of exposure but she realized that it had done untold damage to her trust in Dad's safety and also to her confidence in her own appearance. The rightful umbrella of protection which Jenny's dad should have provided, had been blown away, leaving her hugely exposed, both physically and spiritually. We talked some more and God brought wonderful restoration to Jenny as she forgave her dad and we asked the Lord to re-establish *His* covering over the troubled place in her heart. God then gently dealt with the legacy of anxiety, anger and shame.

Taking time to see the need

A couple of years ago we began to notice the dreadful dilapidation of one of the outbuildings at Ellel Glyndley Manor. The whole team walked past this building regularly and we were all so familiar with its condition that we were blind to just how bad a state it was in. "What a shame!" someone said one day, "It looks such a mess and it could have made an attractive estate office." We realized that we'd let the building fall into serious disrepair. It was barely staying propped up and it was indeed *a shame*. We set about a thorough repair mainly because we felt ashamed at the state of the building. It is now sound and weatherproof and an important asset to the work.

Like that little building, our lives can get into disrepair through neglect, and also by the inevitable traumas of life. The main problem with this structure at Glyndley was that the roof was severely damaged and this had allowed the whole building to deteriorate. Whether through our sin or the sin of others, lack of godly covering in our lives can have exactly the same effect. We find ourselves exposed to a hostile spiritual environment. We become out of line with God, or, as the Bible describes it, bearing iniquity:

> *Our fathers sinned, and are no more;*
> *It is we who have borne their iniquities.*

(Lamentations 5:7)

The associated feelings can be shame, fear, anger and a sense of abandonment. All of these, if unresolved, can lead to spiritual bondage, as well as to emotional and physical disorder. Let's start by looking at the important issue of shame. In the exposure which inevitably results from sin, shame can seem to hang around us like an uncomfortable and very restrictive garment. It is not a covering which God wants us to continue wearing.

The covering of shame

Shame is a powerful feeling which grips the lives of many people. God made us to receive warning signals within us when we sin. We feel a disquieting in our human spirit, caused by a conviction of guilt and the associated emotion of shame. Guilt helps us to recognize our sin. Shame helps us to realize how sin has exposed us. These strong feelings are given by God to motivate us to confession and repentance and thereby receive His cleansing. For most people, physical nakedness in public would be shocking and embarrassing. When we are out of line with God, there is a similar sense of exposure and shame because we are removed from God's covering.

This feeling (if we are willing to acknowledge it) is very unpleasant. But God planned it this way so we would remain uncomfortable until we had a change of heart concerning the sin. If we choose not to face the issue in a godly way, then the guilt and shame will remain with us, albeit pushed aside, as an uncomfortable covering which makes it hard to walk with dignity. These are feelings which the prophet Jeremiah recognized:

> *We lie down in our shame,*
> *And our reproach covers us;*
> *For we have sinned against the LORD our God,*
> *We and our fathers,*
> *From our youth even to this day,*
> *And have not obeyed the voice of the LORD our God.*
>
> (Jeremiah 3:25 NKJV)

The reality is that we have all sinned and it is an ongoing process to bring these issues to God for His forgiveness and healing. As we walk with Him, discovering the truth of our lives, each revelation allows us to shed more of the covering of disgrace and to receive His pardon and His clean clothing.

Shame is not always from our own sin

Despite their best efforts to be right with God, some people continue to feel that they are stuck under a shameful covering. Often they don't feel the fullness of the Lord's joy or the safety of His protection over them. What is this problem and how can it be solved?

There may well be experiences which have left them feeling ashamed, with memories of deep humiliation or extreme vulnerability due not to their own behavior but to the actions of others. Perhaps they had been made to feel inadequate in public or, even more seriously, they had been deeply violated and exposed in some way. Seeking God's forgiveness does not relieve this shame because it is not their own sin, and it can lead to a desperate sense of hopelessness.

Anyone experiencing this type of shame may desperately desire help but fear the pain of more exposure. They may be afraid of close relationships and avoid any thought of intimacy. They may try to avoid being noticed, even for the good things they do. They may find it very difficult to receive praise or enter into times of fun and fellowship, and making eye contact with other people can be hard. It can get to a point where they are seeing life through a "shame filter," expecting this feeling in every circumstance, with no hope of change. With this identity, it is a life which is heavy, grey and joyless. They may finally conclude that, despite what actually happened, *they* must have done something so terribly wicked that they are beyond forgiveness and that they must consider themselves an intrinsically *bad person*.

Of course, the truth is that they are not the one who sinned but they are a victim of sin and exposure by others. They may well have been deeply wounded, but the shame which seems to cover them should not in fact be theirs to carry. This shame actually belongs with the guilty one, the one who sinned and caused the exposure. It is not uncommon for an abused child to feel guilty and ashamed for having been abused when clearly the sin is not theirs but belongs to the abuser. The abuser should have taken the responsibility but, wanting to shift the blame for the sin, often "dumps" the guilt and shame on to the victim. For the abuser it is a way of covering up the truth. The victim, in their desperation to make sense of what has happened, sometimes embraces the lie and carries the burden of the sin. As a result they carry false guilt and false shame.

There was a moment in Jesus' life which will help us to understand what to do with shame like this. At the cross, Jesus willingly took the sin, guilt and shame of anyone who would recognize their need of forgiveness. However, around the cross, there were those who were falsely accusing, abusing and humiliating Jesus. They wanted Him to feel personally ashamed at being hung on a cross, naked and exposed. They were sinning against Him, but they wanted Him to feel ashamed of the exposure, for which they were to blame. The writer to the Hebrews tells us how Jesus dealt with this kind of shame:

> looking unto Jesus, the author and finisher of our faith, who for the joy that was set before Him endured the cross, despising the shame, and has sat down at the right hand of the throne of God.
>
> (Hebrews 12:2 NKJV, my own emphasis added)

The word "despising" means "pushing something away." Jesus refused to carry this shame and guilt which was being wrongly pushed on Him. When a victim of abuse recognizes that he or she has been living under a covering of false shame, they need to do what Jesus did! They need to reject the carrying of this shame and agree with Jesus that it can be released, to be carried by the one who sinned. This does not deny the power of forgiveness, but puts the offence where it rightfully belongs. David recognized the importance of this:

Let my accusers be clothed with dishonor,
And let them cover themselves with their own shame as with a robe.

(Psalm 109:29)

We must be careful not to wear a cloak which does not truthfully belong to us.

Feeling fearful and anxious

There are various reasons why we may be spiritually exposed – our own sin, the sin of others or our own attempts at self-protection. Whatever the reason, whenever we are out of God's order and covering, we will always feel troubled, fearful or anxious. It is not just an emotion but a spiritual awareness deep in the heart. God intended that we would rightfully sense this warning and therefore seek His covering. Jesus knew exactly what it felt like to be threatened by the hostility of the powers of darkness. As He got nearer to the horror of the cross, the enemy closed in through the plans of Judas:

When Jesus had said this, He became troubled in spirit, and testified and said, "Truly, truly, I say to you, that one of you will betray Me."

(John 13:21)

When some people talk about their childhood, they describe it as a time when they felt continually troubled, even if there was no specific abuse. There was just something unsafe about the situation day by day. Actually, deep down we all know whether or not a situation is safe and in godly order. Have you ever been to a Christian meeting and the preacher might be saying the right words but your heart says that the spiritual environment is unsafe and that you need to be on your guard? It is important to acknowledge these feelings and to ask the Lord for discernment as to what spirit is at work. Words can seem right but if they come from a heart that is defiled, the words carry a spirit that is unclean, unsafe and even destructive. When Jesus speaks, every word is literally life-giving:

"It is the Spirit who gives life; the flesh profits nothing; the words that I have spoken to you are spirit and are life."

(John 6:63)

The emotion of fear is essentially a God-given warning bell that we are in danger. Even Jesus experienced such warnings. As the time drew near for Him to be arrested, He said,

"Now My soul has become troubled; and what shall I say, 'Father, save Me from this hour'? But for this purpose I came to this hour."

(John 12:27)

Jesus knew that when He felt unsafe, the answer was to talk to His Dad! This immediately reconfirmed the divine order and covering within the Godhead.

However, if we are ignorant of God's help and we are unable to find safety, then the fear and anxiety can grip us and remain an unresolved problem. This place of fear leaves us spiritually exposed and can affect our lives many years after the incident which brought on the fear. It seems as if a part of us is left in the experience of feeling uncovered, unsafe and anxious. We shall see that Jesus can bring resolution to these places of anxiety when He is allowed to be the covering today which we were unable to receive at the time.

To put it simply, fear can be our servant or our master. Fear rightly warns us of danger in order to motivate us to look for protection. However, if we become overwhelmed for lack of godly covering, fear can then be established as a master, controlling the way we think and act. If, for example, we suffered a violent assault from dad as a child, fear was clearly a rightful response. This was meant to cause us to look for safety, but if no safety was available, we may be left trapped with a fear, which can make it difficult to trust anyone, including God. Proverbs 29:25 says,

The fear of man brings a snare,
But he who trusts in the LORD will be exalted.

Let's summarize what God intends when we face danger in our lives:

- Something unsafe occurs.
- Fearful feelings warn us to look for God's covering.
- We find in Him a place of safety: spiritually, emotionally and physically.
- The fear dissipates.
- We fully recover from the incident.

For many of us, what actually happens is:

- Something unsafe occurs.
- Fearful feelings warn us of the danger.
- We don't know how to find God's covering.
- We try to sort it out ourselves.
- We find no real safety.
- The fear grips us and remains in a place to control our lives.
- The incident remains unresolved.

The answer to dealing with any fear which has a control over our lives is to acknowledge this reality and confess that we have unwittingly given it a place to be a master. The Bible tells us that when we give over this fearful place to the perfect Master, dealing with the reasons why we felt so unsafe, the security of the perfect love of Jesus drives out the fear and brings peace to the whole body: "There is no fear in love; but perfect love casts out fear" (1 John 4:18a). In a later chapter we will look at how we might pray for God's healing from the times of anxiety in our lives.

Feeling angry

Anger is a God-given emotional response to injustice. When, for example, parents do not provide adequate spiritual covering for their children, angry feelings will inevitably grow in the heart of the child, whether these are acknowledged or not. When we are unable to express anger, it becomes buried in a place of spiritual darkness, sometimes exploding to the surface unexpectedly in later life. Anger at injustice is not a sin; however, what we have done with the anger may well cause us to be out of line with God!

Many Christians are walking with buried anger which was caused by the injustice of being spiritually exposed by others during their childhood. At the time, expressing the anger did not seem to be an option, so it got put into store. For many, it has now become a frightening volcanic magma of frustration which they have learned to keep underground. Unfortunately it can erupt without warning and can have devastating consequences for those in the vicinity.

What does the Bible say about anger? In the letter to the Ephesians there is a very direct and profound exhortation from Paul to the Christians:

> *Be angry, and yet do not sin; do not let the sun go down on your anger . .*
>
> (4:26)

In just a few words he explains the problem and points to an answer. Our problem is *not* that we were wrong to be angry when faced with injustice, but that we may have expressed it in ungodly ways or let it get buried in the dark. The solution is that *today* we can confess this wrong and forgive those who perpetrated the injustice. We can let Jesus bring the anger into the light and let it be removed from the place of controlling us and those around us.

I have had some deep issues of anger relating to painful relationships in the past. Like many of us, I had learned to live with the buried angry feelings, but I became more and more aware of the effect which these were having on my life. Unresolved anger can bring significant disorder to the body, including sleeplessness, headaches and depression. I knew it had to be faced. I spoke with trusted friends, and prayed through the issues of forgiveness and confessed my ways of trying to cover up the pain. Then I needed to let the anger out. I went to a nearby beach and threw stones at the breakwaters, while expressing the frustrations which had never been voiced. I was on my own and able to shout without others being affected. I knew for certain that God had heard and that I didn't have to keep it to myself any longer. From that day, it was not going to be a dark place for the enemy to use against me or against those around me.

Feeling abandoned

In John 14:18 Jesus says to His disciples, "I will not leave you as orphans; I will come to you." For some people, the lack of spiritual covering in their lives, particularly through poor fathering, has left them feeling like abandoned orphans deep on the inside. It is not their physical condition which they are describing, but the feelings of intense exposure experienced by their human spirit. Very often they have learned, over the years, to rise up and face life with self-protecting determination. But it can seem as if a part of them still lies cowering in a dark corner.

Although they may have been unwilling to face the issue, for many people there comes a time of exhaustion from all the years of hiding the "orphan" inside. It can be a precious opportunity to take Jesus at His word and let Him come to that seemingly abandoned place. He sees the condition of our human spirit and, like any good shepherd, will happily seek out the lost lamb, caught in the barbed wire. We will look later at ways to pray about these issues. Because covering is a spiritual issue it is not constrained by time. So God is able, today, to find, rescue and recover every part of our lives trapped in a place of isolation and abandonment.

The progression of damage caused by exposure

I referred earlier to the little building in the grounds of Ellel Glyndley Manor. Through our neglect it had got into a serious state of disrepair and was not that far from collapse. Buildings can be exposed to damage for many different reasons, but we have been reminded that it is when the roof is affected by poor maintenance and storms that the structure really starts to suffer. It is the same in our lives. There can be a lack of godly covering, together with specific traumas, which leave the body exposed to dysfunction.

To give a simple picture, let's compare the deterioration of a building, resulting from lack of care and adverse weather, with the similar effect of spiritual exposure on a human life.

For a building:

- A neglected or damaged roof creates a major problem.
- Holes let in the rain.
- The inside of the building gets wet.
- Damp conditions encourage the growth of fungus and pest infestation.
- Fungal growth draws more dampness.
- Rotten wood distorts structural integrity.
- Distortion of the structure leads to more roof damage.
- Patching over the top of the damaged areas just hides the real problem.
- In serious situations the building is heading for collapse.

For the human body:

- A damaged spiritual covering can affect us profoundly.
- Holes in God's protection expose us to spiritual hostility.
- We experience fear, anxiety and shame.
- There is wounding which can lead to sinful beliefs and behaviors.
- The enemy has a place to defile our heart and to promote iniquity.
- Our lives become distorted and we move away from truth.
- We make ungodly decisions that expose us even further.
- We attempt to provide our own protection, but it is worse than useless.
- In serious situations we can be heading for breakdown.

Praise God that it is never too late to call in the Master Builder.

When we are uncovered it is easier to fall into sin

We have seen that uncovered lives are out of line with God. The Bible calls this iniquity. We may not have been responsible for the spiritual exposure but, as is clear from Lamentations 5:7, we can certainly be experiencing the consequences:

> *Our fathers sinned, and are no more:*
> *It is we who have borne their iniquities.*

The writer of Lamentations is looking at the devastation of people's lives and reflecting on the causes. Like the damaged building we have been picturing, God's people are walking in distress which has come from the carelessness of their forebears:

> *Our inheritance has been turned over to strangers,*
> *Our houses to aliens.*
>
> (Lamentations 5:2)

There is despair over what they are suffering, but there is also recognition that the spiritual exposure has given rise to their own personal sin:

> *The joy of our hearts has ceased;*
> *Our dancing has been turned into mourning.*
> *The crown has fallen from our head;*
> *Woe to us, for we have sinned!*
>
> (Lamentations 5:15–16)

Sin leads to spiritual exposure. This is a condition which is out of line with God, a place of iniquity, and this invariably leads to more sin. The sinful patterns which we so often see passed from father to son are not just learned behavior, but the spiritual consequence of a lack of godly covering. It can be the same in a church. It is not uncommon to find that, where there is sin in a congregation of God's people, the same sin started with the leaders.

When we are uncovered we are vulnerable to deception

Jesus describes Satan as the "father of lies." If our lives are out of order through personal sin or because of our relationships with others, we will be poorly covered by the spiritual umbrella which shelters us from the enemy's infiltration. One of Satan's primary means of defilement is through deception. God has equipped His Body with a powerful antidote, the *gift of discernment*. Paul tells us that all the gifts are for the benefit of the Body, acting in harmony:

> *But to each one is given the manifestation of the Spirit for the common good.*
>
> (1 Corinthians 12:7)

We are very dependent on God's gifting in one another for the well-being of the whole Body, including our own protection from deception. It is as we together weigh and test teaching, prophecy and ministry that we can walk in a safe place, sheltered from the enemy's lies. It is so important that we search Scripture together and listen to the wisdom of God through our brothers and sisters in the Lord. Particular responsibility rests with those who hold up God's covering umbrella as leaders or teachers. Those who walk in independence, arrogance or pride, ignoring godly order, will invariably stray into deception and take others with them. When deception is empowered by a lack of godly confrontation it soon turns to delusion.

These are very challenging days for each of us to desire earnestly the gift of discernment for God's people. According to Jesus, there will be more and more false and seductive spirituality in these last days. Those in God's family are safe when they are walking in right relationship with Jesus and with each other, covered and protected from the increasingly subtle lies of the enemy.

When we are uncovered things can get broken

We saw earlier that the trauma of physical, emotional and spiritual exposure can be so profound as to cause complete overwhelm and even brokenness on the inside of our lives. Let's look at this a little more closely. We know from the Bible that this kind of fracture is possible because Jesus said that His calling included restoring the broken-hearted:

> *"The Spirit of the Lord is upon Me,*
> *because He has anointed Me*
> *To preach the gospel to the poor,*
> *He has sent Me to heal the brokenhearted . . . "*
>
> (Luke 4:18 NKJV)

What does this brokenness mean? A literal translation of the Hebrew word used by Isaiah (quoted above by Jesus) means that the heart has been shattered into pieces. The heart is composed of the soul (mind, will and emotions) and the human spirit. In violent storms, parts of a building can get disconnected from other parts; the structure can get seriously damaged and distorted. Cables and communications may be severed. Someone could be shouting for help in the basement but no one else in the building would be able to hear!

The same can happen to us. We are complex creations of God: body, soul and spirit. The man who was stripped, robbed and traumatized in the story of the Good Samaritan is described as being left by the side of the road "half dead." The consequence of serious incidents in our lives can be that we become emotionally and spiritually disconnected with the part of us which suffered the impact of what happened. This can trap the painful feelings in the disconnected place. Sometimes people can lose all memory of the incident but they know that they are still being affected by the trauma because they are experiencing pains, anxieties, depression, etc.

If God says that He seeks to repair brokenness, then clearly this condition lies outside His perfect order for our lives. An airplane with cracks in the fuselage would be recognized as seriously compromised in its integrity and safety and very vulnerable to the pressures of flight. When our hearts have been broken by traumatic events, we become further exposed to the spiritual hostility of the world around us. Brokenness is a vulnerable place and God desires that we be re-covered and brought to safety, just like the man who had been left for dead in the story of the Good Samaritan.

Storms damage buildings and damaged buildings are then even more susceptible to the next storm! It is not unusual to find that those who have experienced an accident or trauma early in life seem more susceptible to similar incidents throughout their lives. When someone says, "I am accident prone," it is well worth seeking to understand how they first got uncovered.

Let me tell you about Pat. Due to the carelessness of her parents, she fell off a balcony at the age of two. She had lived for nearly fifty years with deep but unspecific anxieties and head pains, ever since the time of the accident. We had the privilege of praying with her and she forgave those who had been careless with her safety. We asked the Lord to repair the broken heart which had occurred at the time of the fall. Pat was marvelously restored and experienced an amazing new sense of peace and safety on the inside. Her physical condition also dramatically improved.

When a plate is carelessly dropped on the floor, the resulting damage may not be very obvious but, if there is a crack, the plate will have lost the pleasant ringing sound when tapped with a finger. There is a deadness to the sound which it makes. In addition to this, however small the crack appears, it will inevitably be the place where dirt gets in. In the places in our lives which have been uncovered, traumatized and left in emotional distress and broken-ness, there will be spiritual deadness and probably dirt from the enemy.

When we are uncovered the enemy can get a grip

We have established that spiritual territory which is not in God's order and under His covering, is not neutral territory. The enemy lays claim. The consequences of spiritual exposure are not just emotional and physical damage but also spiritual captivity. A place which lacks God's covering is not a place of *no covering* but a place in spiritual darkness. We need to remember that, like many thieves, the enemy really does operate under cover of darkness.

While we were praying for Pat, who fell off the balcony, we realized that the enemy had taken specific advantage of this unprotected and traumatic moment in her life. She explained how subsequently she had been affected by many life-threatening accidents. We began to discern that the enemy had laid particular claim to her life because of the sinful lack of godly parental protection and the spiritual exposure caused by the serious fall. As we prayed with her, we commanded the spirit of death to leave the place of brokenness and trauma. There was a quiet, but very clear, deliverance. We proclaimed that God was re-covering her, giving her life in abundance. Pat looked radiant as she described the restoring of a deep peace to her body!

God offers a loving shelter to all His creation but His covering can only be received by those who obey Him. Caleb tried to explain this simple principle to the Children of Israel who were afraid to enter the promised land and face the giants who seemed to be threatening them:

> *"Only do not rebel against the LORD; and do not fear the people of the land, for they will be our prey. Their protection has been removed from them, and the LORD is with us; do not fear them."*
>
> (Numbers 14:9)

Giving a place to fear can be an expression of how little we trust God. The Israelites could not fully experience God's covering if they didn't trust Him. They were playing into the enemy's hands.

If we are disobedient to the spiritual authority of God, we fall instead under the authority of Satan, the ruler of this world. He seeks to hold this ground with his demonic forces:

> *And you were dead in your trespasses and sins, in which you formerly walked according to the course of this world, according to the prince of the power of the air, of the spirit that is now working in the sons of disobedience.*
>
> (Ephesians 2:1–2)

Ezekiel shares God's heart as he declares the consequence of the bad shepherding of God's people, who have been left uncovered, scattered and vulnerable to the enemy's desire to devour them:

> *They were scattered for lack of a shepherd, and they became food for every beast of the field and were scattered.*

> (Ezekiel 34:5)

Sinful shepherds, idolatrous forebears, our own sinful actions and our attempts at self-covering the painful places can all expose us to the rule of the enemy, instead of the protection of God. If we don't fully appropriate the restoring work of Jesus, we may live (at least in part) as slaves to a destructive master rather than children of a loving Father.

For whatever reason, we have all experienced situations in our lives when God's covering was not in place. These times bring spiritual darkness and give the enemy rights or authority. Depending on the circumstances, this ungodly authority may have been strengthened by demonic power and this defiles our lives. A Christian is not automatically released from the effects of spiritual darkness when he or she is born again into God's kingdom, in the same way that a sea bird is not completely clean when removed from an oil spill.

One could say that our spiritual location at rebirth changes dramatically from darkness to light, but the spiritual residue can take a while to deal with! We carry this spiritual residue from the uncovered times of our lives and these can result in bondage today, which only Jesus can release. He came to set captives free and we can invite Him into any unresolved situation in our lives. As we follow His commands, His authority is established and the enemy has to retreat.

Unclean spirits promoting fear, isolation, anger, feelings of an orphan, shame and infirmity may need to be addressed and evicted. When Jesus is welcomed in, the enemy has to move out! As an example of how the enemy gets a hold, we noted earlier, in Ephesians chapter 4, how the writer encourages Christians to be careful not to bury anger:

Be angry, and yet do not sin; do not let the sun go down on your anger, and do not give the devil an opportunity.

(vv. 26–27)

Anything which is left in the dark remains unresolved and can be damaging to us. It is never too late to let *the* Light in!

When we are uncovered the body does not work properly

Our bodies work through an amazing inter-relationship between the body, the soul and the spirit. Because it is a spiritual issue, lack of godly covering initially affects our human spirit, bringing disorder in our spiritual framework. Our soul then experiences darkness rather than light, so our thinking, feelings and choices become distorted. The enemy can take advantage of this and establish his grip to strengthen the disorder. The physical body responds to the absence of spiritual life by experiencing dysfunction and illness. To summarize, we don't work properly.

Try putting your radio out into the garden for a week or two. It wasn't designed to be left out in the open, and sooner or later it will stop working. The problem will start when rain affects the delicate electrical circuits on the inside. The final result will be that sound will stop coming from the loudspeaker. In the same way, our bodies were not designed to be exposed to a spiritually hostile environment. The dysfunction will start on the inside but eventually our physical bodies just won't work the way God intended.

Let me give an example of how people can be affected. Sheila was enjoying the sunshine around a swimming pool, when suddenly she realized a boy was drowning in front of her. No one else seemed to be willing to help so she dived in and found herself very nearly drowning as well. Still no one came to help as she gasped and struggled to keep her head above water. Eventually she and the boy made it to safety. This had happened to Sheila many years before, but now, as we prayed with her, she experienced very strong feelings of terror and anger as she reflected on how exposed and vulnerable she had felt.

Sheila explained to us that it was from this time that she had started to develop asthma. She realized that her anger was directed at the swimming pool attendants who were not where they should have been. The shepherds were missing. She also realized that, as the situation had increasingly overwhelmed her, she had been gripped by fear and that her lungs had been the focus of that fear. She made a choice to speak out forgiveness towards those who had left her uncovered and God wonderfully stepped into the place of exposure as she was delivered and healed from the fear and the asthma.

Losing our immunity

God designed the human body to be physically guarded from infection through an immune system which detects, and protects the body from, hostile substances and organisms. It is the physical equivalent of God's personal spiritual protection. We see from the Bible that rebellion against God's law and order results in a loss of God's protection over our lives. Deuteronomy 28 says, for example:

> " . . . *if you do not obey the* LORD *your God . . . The* LORD *will smite you with the boils of Egypt and with tumors and with the scab and with the itch, from which you cannot be healed.*"
>
> (vv. 15, 27)

It is very interesting that the persistent disorders which are described in this particular passage are associated with the skin, the most significant of the body's natural protective organs, guarding against potentially damaging substances. The body easily fights off even aggressive organisms like MRSA until the skin covering is punctured by wounding or surgery. Actually, every part of our body can come into contact with hostile organisms and chemicals, so we really need this amazing protective system to function as God intended.

The immune system in people's lives can malfunction in several ways including inadequate immunity as well as hypersensitivity (allergic and intolerant reactions). The symptoms can include skin conditions, breathing and digestive disorders, but we need to remember that physical well-being is very often a reflection of our spiritual health. The sage who coined the following proverb alerts us to this truth:

> A joyful heart is good medicine,
> but a broken spirit dries up the bones.

(Proverbs 17:22)

The marrow in our bones is the origin of many of the cells which participate in the body's immune system. When our spiritual immunity is distorted through a lack of God's covering, our body may respond with dysfunction in its ability to guard against the physical environment.

A man, we shall call Clive, was visiting an Ellel Ministries center with his wife. During some teaching on relationships he was convicted by God about his sexual practices with his wife. They had been engaging in oral sex over a number of years and God challenged him to see this as dishonoring to their bodies. As he confessed the practice, he became convinced that God was showing him that this was a spiritual issue with physical consequences, in particular affecting his digestive system. For several years, he and his wife had both been experiencing the same serious food intolerances, causing huge difficulties. The result of the time of prayer was that they were both wonderfully delivered from the hold of this disorder.

Our bodies are designed to react automatically to things which might physically harm us. However, this response system, meant to protect us, can be distorted if our lives have been spiritually exposed through wounding or sin issues, including our attempts to provide our own covering.

Summary

Being out of God's covering affects our lives, inside and outside. We can be carrying today the consequence of spiritual exposure from the present, or from many years ago. Deep feelings such as anxiety, shame, anger and abandonment can very often relate to unresolved times of wounding from the past, where God's covering was not in place.

The Bible calls it iniquity when we are out of line with God, for whatever reason. One way of describing this is that it is like wearing dirty clothes that God longs to replace with clean garments.

He spoke and said to those who were standing before him, saying, "Remove the filthy garments from him." Again he said to him, "See, I have taken your iniquity away from you and will clothe you with festal robes."

(Zechariah 3:4)

Just like a building which suffers progressive deterioration when the roof has been damaged, every part of our being can experience disorder without God's covering. This can then make us more vulnerable to the storms of life. Sin issues and severe traumas can cause brokenness in the soul and spirit. These situations all give opportunities to the enemy to take a spiritual hold on our lives and this can be empowered by demons. The physical body reflects the condition of the heart, so the disorder inside very often leads to physical infirmities.

Many people love to restore dilapidated buildings even where the roof has been damaged for a long time. God really loves to restore lives where His covering has been missing over the years. But we must remember that restoration is only possible because of the love, truth and grace of Jesus.

CHAPTER 9

Jesus – the One who covers

It's all about Jesus!

We have looked at the importance of godly law and order as being the place of God's covering. Recognizing the truth of God's Law reveals how we have become spiritually exposed. Recognizing the truth of Jesus reveals how we get re-covered:

> *Therefore the Law has become our tutor to lead us to Christ, so that we may be justified by faith.*
>
> (Galatians 3:24)

God the Father promised, by covenant, that He would cover and heal His people. Jesus has established a new era for this covenant, which can make God's promise a reality for each of us today: "For as many as are the promises of God, in Him [Jesus] they are yes" (2 Corinthians 1:20a).

John Bunyan summed up the centrality of Jesus very well in Part Two of *Pilgrim's Progress*. A character called Great-Heart explains to Christiana: "So then, to speak to the question more at large, the pardon that you have attained was obtained by another, to wit, by Him that let you in at the gate: He [Jesus] has performed righteousness to cover you and spilt blood to wash you in." Jesus *is* the source of true covering and healing. He *is* the strong tower, the robe of righteousness, the guardian of our souls, the caring friend, the perfect father, the loving husband, the king, the good shepherd and the source of the sacrificial blood which has permitted God's mercy. If we truly want to live under God's covering, then we must follow God's commandments, which are actually very simple. The apostle John explains them succinctly in 1 John 3:23–24:

> *This is His commandment, that we believe in the name of His son Jesus Christ, and love one another, just as He commanded us. The one who keeps His commandments abides in Him, and He in him. We know by this that He abides in us, by the Spirit whom He has given us.*

Let me summarize the extraordinary truth expressed in these two verses. To be in covenant with God we must follow His commands. These commands are that we believe wholeheartedly in Jesus Christ and love all those around us. If we do this we will be living in Jesus. At the same time He will be living in us. Jesus is able to do this by the Holy Spirit. Living in Jesus must surely be the best covering possible and, through faith in Him, we can experience this now.

Only Jesus can recover our lives

There is a remarkable story, told by the disciple John, about Jesus stepping into the life of a woman who was very exposed and likely to die from the exposure. It is in John chapter 8 and describes a woman caught in the act of adultery. She is dragged by her accusers into the temple area in front of Jesus. It is very clear in the story that the religious leaders involved are, in effect, representing Satan, as he attempts both to trap Jesus and to destroy the woman.

The whole situation is like a court room where the prosecution lawyer believes that he has an open-and-shut case. There is no doubt that the woman is guilty and that the law declares the punishment to be execution. They ask Jesus for His viewpoint. Surely the woman is doomed to death now that she has been exposed, but Jesus speaks a different verdict. The prosecution is given a choice. Justice can be met by their analysis, in which case they also, as sinners, will be liable for punishment, *or* justice can be met by Him in a completely new way.

This was not at all what the prosecution intended and they decided to leave. The enemy's authority in the courtroom dissipated as the authority of Jesus was established. From a hopeless situation Jesus provided extraordinary protection and freedom for the accused woman, but He did not deny the seriousness of what had happened as He declared to her, "Go, but do not sin any more." Whatever our sin and wounding from the past, Jesus can do the same for us today as He did for that woman. Jesus is able to step in and recover the most hopeless of situations, because He can meet the demands of God's justice on our behalf.

When we were small children we were dependent on our mum and dad making sure that the whole family was kept right with the laws of the country. We did not have the ability to do it on our own. When we take a step of faith and receive Jesus as the Lord of our lives, we become God's children. The great news is that He has made sure that all of God's family are right with His spiritual laws. What a relief!

From extreme exposure to miraculous recovery

Jesus will go to any lengths to seek out those who have been left exposed and in need of His covering. We don't know why the man in the Gerasene region was so seriously affected by demons but the story gives us an assurance that Jesus understands and has compassion on the most broken and defiled of lives. The story is told in both Mark chapter 5 and Luke chapter 8. By looking at these two accounts we can see the full extent of the truly remarkable change in the man's life. Here's a summary of what happened to him. In fact it describes the amazing difference which God's covering can make:

- Before, he was in pain; afterwards, he was at ease.
- Before, he was troubled; afterwards, he was in his right mind.

- Before, he was in bondage; afterwards, he was liberated.
- Before, he was without rest; afterwards, he was seated.
- Before, he was self-harming; afterwards, he was self-respecting.
- Before, he was rejected; afterwards, he was accepted.
- Before, he was alone; afterwards, he was in fellowship.
- Before, he was ashamed; afterwards, he had dignity.
- Before, he was fearful; afterwards, he was at peace.
- Before, he was worthless; afterwards, he was of value.
- Before, he was condemned; afterwards, he was released.
- Before, he was like an animal; afterwards, he was truly human.
- Before, he was directed by demons; afterwards, he was directed by Jesus.

In summary, before Jesus arrived, the man was spiritually and physically naked; afterwards, he was clothed.

Jesus is our covenant representative

Jesus is the *go-between* for all God's promises. He is the guarantor of God's covenant and God's covering. We can only be restored into the friendship God desires to have with us because the Father found a perfect representative for man. Adam was spiritually exposed through breaking covenant with God. After that, the only way that the fullness of God's covering could be restored was if a new covenant agreement could be completely honored by man. The problem was that all men have rebelled against God's commands, but, thankfully, just One remained sinless.

Binding covenants in biblical times were often made by one person representing each member of the group or family entering into the alliance. David and Jonathan made a covenant with each other. It was Jonathan's son, Mephibosheth, who later found that King David felt compelled to honor the vows he had made to all those whom Jonathan had represented. Mephibosheth joined in the blessings of the covenant because he belonged to Jonathan:

David said to him [Mephibosheth], "Do not fear, for I will surely show
kindness to you for the sake of your father Jonathan, and will restore
to you all the land of your grandfather Saul; and you shall eat at my
table regularly."

(2 Samuel 9:7)

Joined to Adam we remain part of a broken covenant. Joined to
Jesus we become part of a fulfilled covenant. For every covenant,
vows and oaths were spoken and animal sacrifices often made to
confirm the life and death nature of the agreement. Uniquely in
history, Jesus perfectly represented God and perfectly represented
mankind (including you and me) as He provided a new covenant
sacrifice at the cross. Amazingly, God is compelled to honor that
covenant towards each of us, when He sees that we are joined to
Jesus and part of His family. At the beginning of his gospel, the
apostle John writes:

But as many as received Him [Jesus], to them He gave the right to
become children of God, even to those who believe in His name.

(1:12)

The more we walk in covenant with God, the more we experience
His spiritual covering.

Whether we acknowledge it or not, we have always needed a hiding
place in this spiritually hostile world. Jesus has provided the answer.
If we receive Jesus as Lord, we are born again into God's family and
Jesus becomes *our* family representative. Just as Mephibosheth was
in his father when Jonathan made covenant with David, we were *in*
Christ when He renewed man's covenant with God and died for our
sin. The Holy Spirit is the One who joins us into Jesus and restores
God's covering. In Colossians 3:3 Paul writes, "For you have died and
your life is hidden with Christ in God."

Jesus told His disciples that He would not leave them as orphans
and He was true to His word. It doesn't matter how badly we have
been exposed by our earthly parents, God is ready to take us under
His protection:

For my father and my mother have forsaken me,
But the Lord will take me up.

(Psalm 27:10)

Jesus is the Good Shepherd

God knew that He would one day have to provide a True Shepherd for His people. Through Ezekiel, He makes known His anger against the shepherds to whom He entrusted the protection of the sheep. Because of their neglect, the flock had become scattered, damaged and trapped. God made a promise to act:

> *For thus says the Lord God, "Behold, I Myself will search for My sheep and seek them out. As a shepherd cares for his herd in the day when he is among his scattered sheep, so I will care for My sheep and I will deliver them from all the places to which they were scattered on a cloudy and gloomy day."*

(Ezekiel 34:11)

Jesus acknowledges that He is that divine Shepherd:

> *"I am the good shepherd, and I know My own and My own know Me, even as the Father knows Me and I know the Father; and I lay down My life for the sheep."*

(John 10:14–15)

Only Jesus can provide the food and shelter which we so desperately need in a world of increasing spiritual famine and darkness.

Jesus is the source of new spiritual clothing

Paul encourages us to *put on* Jesus in our search for the right spiritual protection against the sinful enticements of this world:

> *Let us behave properly as in the day, not in carousing and drunken-ness, not in sexual promiscuity and sensuality, not in strife and*

jealousy. But put on the Lord Jesus Christ, and make no provision for the flesh in regard to its lusts.

(Romans 13:13–14)

Being clothed in Jesus is the consequence of rejecting the ruler of this world and immersing our lives under God's authority. In his letter to the Galatians, Paul emphasizes this truth:

For all of you who were baptized into Christ have clothed yourselves with Christ.

(3:27)

Jesus has paid the price for us to be clothed and covered; the Holy Spirit is the garment whom Jesus has sent. He is a unique covering, promised by God, to bring not just protection but power against the enemy. Shortly before His death, Jesus told His disciples:

"And behold, I am sending forth the promise of My Father upon you; but you are to stay in the city until you are clothed with power from on high."

(Luke 24:49)

Jesus describes Himself as being the Truth:

Jesus said to him, "I am the way, and the truth, and the life; no one comes to the Father but through Me."

(John 14:6)

The belt of truth is one of the items of armor which Paul encourages us to wear in the well-known passage in Ephesians 6:10–18. In fact this protective armor of God is clearly Jesus Himself: our Truth, Righteousness, Peace, Faith and Salvation. These verses describe exposure to the hostility of the enemy as being like flaming arrows. I am very glad that God's covering is much stronger than the umbrella we have previously used as a picture of God's covering. Armor seems a lot more appropriate in most of life's circumstances!

Jesus is the provider of a new spiritual dwelling

In times of war, and particularly where there is enemy occupation, *safe houses* are critical for the survival of those resisting the foreign oppression. In this world, most people have unknowingly chosen collaboration with the ruling powers. Christians are in support of the rightful King, but the enemy is constantly on the prowl. Jesus offers Himself and His love as a safe house:

> "*Just as the Father has loved Me, I have also loved you; abide in my love.*"
>
> (John 15:9)

What an offer!

How do we find this safe place to live? Jesus explains:

> "*If you keep My commandments, you will abide in My love; just as I have kept My Father's commandments and abide in His love.*"
>
> (John 15:10)

Members of a resistance movement need to know whom they can trust. We need to get to know the voice of Jesus so that we can be sure to follow His commands.

In these verses from the Gospel of John, Jesus encourages us to abide in Him, in the context of wanting us to enjoy fruitful lives. He elsewhere reminds us that, in order to get fruit, there often needs to be drastic pruning. He is telling us that there are likely to be beliefs and behaviors in our lives which can't be under the same roof as Him. He is ready to show us these, so that we can bear much fruit:

> "*If you abide in Me, and My words abide in you, ask whatever you wish, and it will be done for you. My Father is glorified by this, that you bear much fruit, and so prove to be My disciples.*"
>
> (John 15:7–8)

The need for Jesus' blood

Announcing the words "I am covered by the blood of Jesus" will never by itself restore divine protection. Only our relationship with Jesus re-establishes God's covering in our lives. Having said that, the blood of Jesus is staggeringly powerful. Even animal sacrifice, when it was done in obedience to the commands of God, totally disarmed destructive forces. One of the most powerful examples of this is when, in the face of persistent stubbornness by Egypt's pharaoh who refused to release the Israelites from their slavery in his land, the Lord sends the angel of death to strike down the first-born in every family:

> *"For the LORD will pass through to smite the Egyptians; and when He sees the blood on the lintel and on the two doorposts, the LORD will pass over the door and will not allow the destroyer to come into your houses to smite you."*
>
> (Exodus 12:23)

Sin is so serious that the only just consequence is death. God has clearly identified sacrificial blood with the meeting of His justice and the release of His pardon and covering to His people:

> *"For the life of the flesh is in the blood, and I have given it to you on the altar to make atonement for your souls; for it is the blood by reason of the life that makes atonement."*
>
> (Leviticus 17:11)

Remember *atonement* literally means the restoring of God's covering. In other words, to be covered by God requires the shedding of sacrificial blood. The instructions under the Old Covenant were for repeated animal sacrifices. But under the New Covenant, only the blood of Jesus is sufficient. When the blood of Jesus is evident, God's justice has been met, His pardon is declared, and the enemy is forced to back off.

The important thing for the Israelites was that this divine protection was only effective for them if they followed God's instructions. Obedience to God's commands brings His covering, not just the voicing of His truth. We are hidden with Christ and covered by His blood only by virtue of our relationship of obedience to Him. It would foolish, for example, to plead the covering of the blood of Jesus in some difficult situation, while walking in known rebellion to God's commandments.

The testimony of our being a follower of Jesus is not just our words, but also the attitudes and actions which prove our words. When Satan recognizes true surrender to the authority of Jesus, he is indeed restrained by the shed blood of Jesus. Transported into heaven in a vision, the apostle John hears a loud voice cry out:

> *"And they overcame him because of the blood of the Lamb and because of the word of their testimony, and they did not love their life even when faced with death."*

> (Revelation 12:11)

When the truth about the blood of Jesus is declared in words and actions, the enemy can't stand it, because it is the reason why he has lost spiritual authority!

Where the powers of darkness still hold some ground in people's lives, teaching on the importance of the blood of Jesus can cause surprisingly hostile responses. Sometimes people will get up out of their seats and run for the door. This is not a new problem. Jesus was one day explaining the importance of His disciples being intimately joined to Him. He described it as being the same as eating His body and drinking His blood. It was at that point that most of His followers left:

> *"He who eats My flesh and drinks My blood abides in Me, and I in him"* . . . *As a result of this many of His disciples withdrew and were not walking with Him anymore.*

> (John 6:56, 66)

The Way, the Truth and the Life

In John chapter 14, Jesus declares Himself to be "the way, the truth and the life." The statement implies a progression, with a goal of abundant life.

Like the disciples who abandoned Jesus, we may not always find the words of Jesus comfortable to hear, especially when He points to the reasons for spiritual exposure in our lives. However, He *is* absolute truth. We certainly want the abundant *life* which He offers and we are probably willing to recognize Jesus as the only *way* to get there. However, there is a doorway of *truth* which cannot be avoided if we are to reach the life of freedom and wholeness which comes when we are right with God.

This doorway involves facing the truth about the way we live our lives and our relationship with God. The only people whom Jesus seemed unable to help were those who were living a life of pretence. Jesus called them hypocrites. My children often used to say to me, "Get real, dad." It was good advice.

In the next chapter we are going to see how to appropriate God's covering and healing. The process of divine recovery starts with a love relationship with Jesus (the way), followed by progressive revelation about Him and about our lives (the truth), leading to spiritual and physical restoration (the life). With new wholeness and freedom, we actually find ourselves in a deeper place of intimacy with Jesus, again discovering more truth and more opportunity for healing. It is a precious journey of growing relationship with God and it takes a lifetime. The enemy will do all he can to interrupt that journey, especially by trying to keep us in the dark, the only realm in which he has any authority.

Summary

Ever since the Fall, Father God has wanted us to be fully sheltered again by Him. He wants us to enjoy the benefits of that divine protection. This was the essence of His covenant promise to Abraham and to all his descendants. Time and time again God spelt it out to

His people through His spokesmen, saying, for example, through Jeremiah:

> *"But this is what I commanded them, saying, 'Obey My voice, and I will be your God, and you will be My people; and you will walk in all the way which I command you, that it may be well with you.'"*
>
> (Jeremiah 7:23)

Jesus walked the earth as a perfect representative of man, fully obeying the Father's commands. In this way, Jesus has re-established the covenant promise on behalf of all of God's family. As Jesus hung on the cross He sealed God's forgiveness, covenant and covering for those who want to be in that family. Receiving Jesus as Lord joins us to Him and to God's everlasting covenant of protection and provision:

> *And if you belong to Christ, then you are Abraham's descendants, and heirs according to promise.*
>
> (Galatians 3:29)

This supernatural process is the work of the Holy Spirit. He is the One who puts into effect the reality of God's ultimate and perfect covering, which is to be *in Christ.*

As we live more in Him, we can know more of His healing power, which actually comes when He is more in us. Jesus said,

> *"In that day you will know that I am in My Father, and you in Me, and I in you."*
>
> (John 14:20)

A bottle in the sea is not fully immersed until it gradually tips over and becomes full of sea water. Let's make sure that no part of our life has been left out of this promise of Jesus, that we can be fully in Him, and He can be fully in us.

CHAPTER 10

Getting covered

A time for healing

The need for recovery

We can suffer from too much sun or too much rain. Either way it's because we were not sufficiently protected. I mentioned earlier how, on one of my camping exploits, I lost a tent in a storm on the Scottish mountains. I also remember in the early days of sleeping under canvas, often waking up in the morning to find that the bottom of my sleeping bag had spent many hours outside the tent, experiencing overnight rain. As I came out of my sleep, most of me was snug and warm but the message from my feet was that a part of me was not at all happy!

When we talk to the Lord about our lives and our need of healing today, He may well want to show us something. It may be that a part of us is suffering from the effects of a time when we were out of His covering. Remember that this is a spiritual issue and will not be resolved by the passing of time, but only by our response to God's commands. Jesus has called us to dwell in Him increasingly and to lead fruitful lives:

> *"I am the vine, you are the branches; he who abides in Me and I in him, he bears much fruit, for apart from Me you can do nothing."*
>
> (John 15:5)

Today's storms expose poor maintenance

Many people begin to look for help in their lives because they experience storms today which have exposed the weaknesses of the past. Poor roofing can remain undetected for years until the gales hit town. The disciple Peter was doing fine until the arrest of Jesus shattered his world and exposed the deep fears which had been covered up. When he denied Jesus to a servant girl, Peter just added lies to the unreality which had been his fig leaves. Jesus had warned him that what was hidden would be brought to the surface:

> *"Simon, Simon, behold, Satan has demanded permission to sift you like wheat . . . "*
>
> (Luke 22:31)

There is a wonderful conclusion to this story. Jesus restored and re-covered Peter from his despair early one morning, walking on a beach. Once Peter got real with Jesus, he could move right into his destiny:

> *He [Jesus] said to him [Peter] a second time, "Simon, son of John, do you love Me?" . . . He [Jesus] said to him [Peter], "Shepherd My sheep."*
>
> (John 21:16)

It's never too late to get covered

When, in the seventies, my wife and I purchased the old farmhouse in the Highlands of Scotland, it had been unoccupied for a considerable time and it desperately needed new owners with vision to restore this remote dwelling. We realized that it would be a substantial challenge. On the day of the handover we were excited but naively unaware of what lay ahead. The change of ownership only took an hour or so, but we were soon to discover that the restoration would take years.

As I investigated more closely the sturdy stone and slate building, I soon found evidence of a long history of problems from storms and neglect. The fierce Highland gales had clearly damaged the roof on many occasions. Ineffective repairs and rotten rafters showed how poor the maintenance had been over the years. Nevertheless I eagerly explored every part of our new acquisition and little by little completed restoration to the roofing and to the damage inside. Actually, I loved every minute of the work.

When you and I were purchased, or redeemed, back from the enemy, God could see the damage in our lives. Restored into covenant relationship with Him, it is His delight to search us and to reinstate His full covering over us and His right order within us. It is never too late to work with Him in this process.

We are going to look at how He does this.

God loves to hear us say that we need Him and trust Him

Hezekiah was a good king, a good leader and a good shepherd of God's people. He saw clearly that, for generations, they had broken covenant with God and were now reaping the consequence:

> *"For our fathers have been unfaithful and have done evil in the sight of the LORD our God, and have forsaken Him and turned their faces away from the dwelling place of the LORD, and have turned their backs."*

(2 Chronicles 29:6)

He resolved to address the problem and to deal with the restoration of the temple, the house of the Lord, recognizing that the people desperately needed to be back in right relationship with God:

> *"Now it is in my heart to make a covenant with the LORD God of Israel, that His burning anger may turn away from us."*

(2 Chronicles 29:10)

He carefully organized the people to put right all that had been neglected in their own lives and in the temple worship. It was a major undertaking and some of the prescribed rituals were missed in the enthusiasm. Eventually, having got to a point where he felt that he had done all he could to prepare the ground for God's work of restoration, Hezekiah prayed for the people:

> *"May the good* Lord *pardon [kaphar, cover] everyone who prepares his heart to seek God, the* Lord *God of his fathers, [even] though [it is] not according to the purification rules of the sanctuary." So the* Lord *heard Hezekiah and healed the people.*
>
> (2 Chronicles 30:18b–20)

There isn't a formula. If our hearts are right and we are honestly seeking to be back under God's covering, He is only too ready to respond and bring His healing. God encourages us to remind Him that He has bound himself to His covenant promises:

> *"I, even I, am the one who wipes out your transgressions*
>   *for My own sake,*
> *And I will not remember your sins.*
> *Put Me in remembrance, let us argue our case together;*
> *State your cause, that you may be proved right."*
>
> (Isaiah 43:25–26)

Nakedness can be a bit embarrassing. It is not easy to let God see the exposed places in our lives. Actually, of course, He has already seen them!

Disciples of Jesus should help to clothe the naked

It has always been one of God's commands to His people to clothe the naked:

> *"Is this not the fast which I choose,*
> *To loosen the bonds of wickedness . . .*

When you see the naked, to cover him;
And not to hide yourself from your own flesh?"

(Isaiah 58:6, 7)

Jesus commands the same to His disciples, explaining that He is personally affected by their obedience. As usual, they find it difficult to see His meaning:

" . . . *when did we see You a stranger, and invite You in, or naked, and clothe You? When did we see You sick, or in prison, and come to You?" The King will answer and say to them, 'Truly I say to you, to the extent that you did it to one of these brothers of Mine, even the least of them, you did it to Me.' "*

(Matthew 25:38, 40)

Jesus provides the only way for mankind to find the spiritual clothing which they have lost through disobedience to God's commands. Through the outpouring of the Holy Spirit, Jesus has delegated the ministry of recovery to His followers. Of course, it is still God who does the re-covering but He has called His disciples to be instruments of His plans for restoration. Christians who are looking for recovery from the wounding which life brings will often need the help of other brothers and sisters in the Body of Christ. As they become stronger they can then assist others.

Who cares?

Let me refer again to one of the best-known stories of recovery in the Bible. It is the rescue and restoration of a man attacked on the road from Jerusalem to Jericho. In Luke chapter 10, Jesus tells this story to highlight the compassion which should be in the heart of His followers towards those who have become exposed and damaged.

The man in the story is literally left naked, half dead, abandoned and in desperate need of help. Two religious men pass by without helping but, shockingly for the people listening to Jesus, help comes from a Samaritan. The rescuer goes to the scene of the trauma and gives immediate first aid, covering the wounded places. But he doesn't stop there. The injured man would still be very exposed to danger if he were to be left at the side of the road. The Samaritan takes the man away from the scene of the attack to a place which will allow the recovery to be completed.

What an amazing picture of God's way of restoring lives which have been wrecked by all the various kinds of damage experienced by each of us on life's journey. Let me summarize how it is done. We need God's help, often through others. God uses ordinary and sometimes unlikely people like you and me, who have the heart of Jesus for hurting people. He equips us, both to see how lives have been damaged and also to understand how to apply God's first aid. The fullness of healing for the wounded person comes only when a safe shelter is found, where Jesus has paid the full price for their recovery.

This *is* the healing ministry of Jesus in which He has called His followers to participate. At the end of the story which is usually entitled the Good Samaritan, Jesus says to those listening, and particularly to the inquisitive lawyer, "Go and do the same."

Exposing what has been wrongly covered

We do not need to strive. God's heart is to bring light into dark places. The Pharisees around Jesus were typical of those who kept their sinful hearts covered up. As God is allowed to have His way, the enemy is exposed whether he likes it or not! Jesus told His disciples:

> *"Beware of the leaven of the Pharisees, which is hypocrisy. But there is nothing covered up that will not be revealed, and hidden, that will not be known."*

(Luke 12:1b–2)

All sorts of things come to light when Jesus is given access to our lives. It may be our own sin. It may be the abuse of others. It may be traumatic incidents. It may be years of feeling unsafe. It may be things which we have tried to forget. It may be things which God suddenly brings back to our minds. We may get in touch with anxiety, shame, anger or despair. We may realize for the first time that our physical dysfunction is rooted in the uncovered times. We may just realize how exhausted we have become with trying to cover up the pain for so long. When God reveals, He simply waits for us to respond in agreement with Him and His view of our lives.

A prayer journey of recovery

Let's look at some steps to restore God's precious spiritual covering over places in our lives where there have been times of exposure and wounding. We can ask Him to highlight these times and direct the prayers. It is very often good to share these steps with brothers or sisters in Christ. They can agree with us, encourage us and stand with us against the enemy's hold on our lives.

This was the principle that Jesus adopted when He sent out the disciples in twos, to teach, heal and deliver those in need. At Ellel Ministries centers, our normal practice is to have two of our team members come alongside each person who requests help and prayer. Usually at least one of the team members would be the same sex as the one receiving ministry. We find that this creates a safe and secure environment.

At each step described below there are suggestions for what you can say. Feel free to put the prayers in your own words. There are also gaps where you can put in specific names or details if you wish.

1. Acknowledge the reality of spiritual exposure
There was a critical moment for the prodigal son when he *came to his senses* and realized just how vulnerable he was feeding pigs, and how safe he *could* be, in his father's house.

Where and when in my life have I been spiritually exposed because God's order was not fully in place? Recognize the emotions, some-times buried, of feeling unsafe, overwhelmed, fearful, abandoned, traumatized or ashamed. Has something been "swept under the carpet" which God is now saying needs to be out in the open? It is time for truth in order to challenge the "father of lies," as Jesus calls Satan. Ask God to reveal truth.

Was the lack of godly covering over a period of time or was it one particular incident? Was there an umbrella with serious holes or was there no umbrella at all? Recognize that any exposure causes damage – spiritual, emotional and physical.

A suggestion for what to say:

> Father God, I confess [agree with You] that there has been a time in my life which was not in godly order because of _____ [sin, trauma, lack of care], when I was not fully under Your covering. It is my desire, through Jesus my Lord, to be restored in that part of my life and to receive shelter, freedom and healing for all that was damaged when I was not able to be protected by Your covenant love. Thank You, Father, that You have seen my need.

2. Was I, at least in part, responsible for what happened?

The uncovering of our lives may be through the sin of others, but it may also be, in part, of our own making. Sheep can't always blame the shepherd for things being out of order. They can make a choice to put their heads through a barbed-wire fence, thinking the grass is greener, only to find that they get caught and damaged. We have often been careless with our own lives, through ignorance, fear, lust, rebellion or pride. Going outside the boundaries which God has made for us breaks covenant with Him and leaves us exposed.

We can choose to follow the Spirit or to follow the world. Our sinful, soulish nature draws us towards wrong responses in life and we need to be accountable if we have put ourselves into exposed situations, through carelessness or disobedience.

A suggestion for what to say:

> Father God, I confess that I have, in some measure, been responsible for those parts of my life being spiritually

uncovered and vulnerable to the enemy's domain. I repent of the sinful beliefs and behaviors, in particular _____ that broke covenant with You and took me outside Your safe boundaries. I thank You for Your forgiveness and the opportunity for things to be put right.

3. Are there people, particularly shepherds, who need forgiving?

God has ordained that His covering over our lives is only in place when His order is established. This order includes right relationship in "family" groups at home, at work, at church and even in the nation. God has particularly entrusted shepherds such as dads, mums, pastors, directors and leaders, to be a significant means of His protection over His people. This is never more relevant than in the responsibility God places on parents to watch over and nurture their young children.

All sorts of people have sinned against us, including our forebears who have left us with a defiled spiritual inheritance. Who needs to be forgiven in the circumstances being considered here? Shepherds carry a particular responsibility for the well-being of the sheep in their charge. When we should have been able to depend on them, who has sinned, who has been absent, careless, abusive, selfish or unjust? Unfortunately, there has been a lot of sin among shepherds and God knows it. He declares:

> "Woe to the shepherds who are destroying and scattering the sheep of My pasture!"
>
> (Jeremiah 23:1)

We need to take time to face the reality of the offences against us and reach a decision to forgive all those involved, as Jesus has commanded. It may not be what we feel like doing but it is the only way for us to find true healing. When we release them from the debt which they owe us, we find freedom by the grace of God:

"Whenever you stand praying, forgive, if you have anything against
anyone, so that your Father who is in heaven will also forgive you
your transgressions."

(Mark 11:25)

We cannot find true restoration today, from the abuse of the past,
except by forgiveness. It does not change what happened, but it does
change the condition of our hearts from a place of unrest to a place
of peace.

A suggestion for what to say:

> Father God, I recognize that there have been people in my
> life, particularly shepherds, who have not cared for me as You
> intended. Instead of being a means of Your covering, they
> exposed me to hurt and damage. It is my choice today to forgive
> _____ [their names] and to release them
> into the freedom of my forgiveness. Father God, set me free
> from any ungodly hold which they still have upon my life, in
> Jesus' name.

4. Getting rid of the fig leaves

When we feel spiritually exposed, we naturally try to find a solution.
The anxiety, guilt, shame and pain are all unpleasant, so we are
desperate for an answer. God's way is best but, in the absence of
knowing His covering, we may resort to rebellion, unreality, denial,
withdrawal, controlling behavior, anger, lies, religion, alcohol, drugs,
dissociation, escapism, wrong relationships, suppressing emotions
or hiding ourselves behind a mask.

Even very little children can make wrong responses to the
wounding which they have suffered. Jesus lays the primary blame
clearly with the adult offender, but we may need to confess that
we stumbled, even as children, in the way we dealt with the
pain:

> *"It is inevitable that stumbling blocks come, but woe to him through*
> *whom they come! It would be better for him if a millstone were hung*

*around his neck and he were thrown into the sea, than that he would
cause one of these little ones to stumble."*

(Luke 17:1–2)

In the absence of godly covering and counsel many children are
pushed into sin, in an attempt to cope with painful exposure.

As adults or children, every response which we have made to
self-protect the exposed places in our lives is a covering of fig leaves.
Man-made covering provides no lasting peace and interferes with
God's desire to provide His perfect clothing.

A suggestion for what to say:

> Father God, at a painful or sinful time when I felt unsafe, I
> sought my own covering and it has not been a place of Your
> truth. I now want to face the truth of what happened and walk
> through this with You into freedom and healing. Consciously
> or unconsciously I tried to disconnect with the reality of the
> trauma or sin. I confess to hiding the issues with wrong attitudes
> and wrong behaviors. I now seek Your forgiveness and ask You
> to reconnect me with the truth of what happened and the truth
> of my feelings. I seek the restoration of Your perfect covering
> and Your authority in my life.

5. Dealing with the trapped emotions

When we were spiritually exposed in our lives, there would have
been strong feelings such as fear, shame, anger, pain and isolation.
Very often it was not possible to express these feelings, so we buried
them under the fig leaves. Emotions are given to us by God to
motivate us into a right response at the time of the incident. Burying
emotions puts them into a spiritually dark place which works against
us. We have referred several times to Paul's injunction not to let a
day go past without dealing with our anger:

> *Be angry, and yet do not sin; do not let the sun go down on your anger,
> and do not give the devil an opportunity.*

(Ephesians 4:26–27)

As we remove the fig leaves and receive God's light into the painful places of exposure, we can release the emotions which have been trapped in the dark. We no longer have to carry the feeling of shame, for example. If it is shame from our own sin we can receive God's forgiveness and freedom. If it is the humiliating shame which has been placed on us by the abuser, it is time to put the shame back in its right place. God promises:

> *Instead of your shame you will have a double portion,*
> *And instead of humiliation they will shout for joy over*
>   *their portion.*

                                                    (Isaiah 61:7)

We need to give ourselves permission to express today all the feelings which could not be expressed when we were uncovered and unsafe. It can take a little while to get in touch with how we really felt. As Joseph became reunited with his brothers it took some time before he could openly face them and touch the truth of how they had all exposed and wounded him so deeply. Finally there came the moment when all the pain came to the surface:

> *Then Joseph could not control himself before all those who stood before*
> *him, and he cried, "Have everyone go out from me." So there was no*
> *man with him when Joseph made himself known to his brothers. He*
> *wept so loudly that the Egyptians heard it, and the household of*
> *Pharaoh heard of it.*
>
> *(Genesis 45:1–2)*

A suggestion for what to say:

> Father God, today I remove my controlling cover which buried the emotions of what happened to me and I give these feelings over to You. I remove the cloak of shame which rightfully belongs to those who exposed me. I receive Your forgiveness for my own sin and I choose to let go of all the guilt, shame,

anxiety, anger and isolation. Father God, help me to be truthful in how I feel, with no more masks or cover-ups.

6. Let God reinstate His covering

Ultimately the covering which God gives to us is the ability for each one of us to dwell in Christ, the place of light, in every part of our lives. As we have seen, the experiences of life have sometimes over-whelmed us and this can leave part of us shrouded in darkness. The psalmist expresses feelings that many of us would identify with:

> For the enemy has persecuted my soul;
> He has crushed my life to the ground;
> He has made me dwell in dark places, like those who have
>   long been dead.
> Therefore my spirit is overwhelmed [shrouded] within me;
> My heart is appalled within me.
>
> (Psalm 143:3–4)

These prayers which we have been looking at above, open a new door to the Holy Spirit. We can welcome Him to restore the exposed place back under the shelter of Christ Jesus. The Holy Spirit clothes us with the very presence of God. This is the safest place in the universe and the place of perfect fathering and perfect covering. Jesus said,

> "I will ask the Father, and He will give you another Helper, that He may be with you forever; that is the Spirit of truth, whom the world cannot receive, because it does not see Him or know Him, but you know Him because He abides with you and will be in you. I will not leave you as orphans; I will come to you."
>
> (John 14:16–18)

A suggestion for what to say:

Father God, I bring this exposed place in my life before You. The enemy has had spiritual authority where Your covering has been absent. It has been a place of lies and not truth, a place of crookedness and not straightness, a place of death and not life. I welcome You, Lord Jesus, by the clothing of the Holy Spirit, to re-cover this part of my life, so that Your authority can be restored and I can know in a deeper way what it means to be safe in God's family. I receive Your precious covering.

7. Remove the enemy's lies, authority and power

We have seen that there are two realms of spiritual authority: God's light and the enemy's darkness. God is the Creator of all things and in ultimate control, but if His covering is absent in any part of our lives, the enemy takes the right to govern that place. Satan's domain gains a foothold when a part of our lives is covered up in darkness. Paul encourages the Christians in Ephesus to root out these places:

> *Do not participate in the unfruitful deeds of darkness, but instead even expose them . . .*

> (Ephesians 5:11)

The enemy's band of thieves can only operate in the dark. When there is light, these unclean spirits can be removed. God's cover brings truth and light. This means that the enemy's lies and darkness are replaced and any demons can be expelled. Every time we say the Lord's Prayer, we are inviting this change of kingdoms:

> " *'Our Father who is in heaven . . .*
> *Your kingdom come . . .*
> *deliver us from [the] evil [one].*
> *For Yours is the kingdom and the power and the glory forever.'* "

> (Matthew 6:9–10, 13)

God has declared Himself committed to this change of spiritual authority in all those who seek Him.

> *. . . on this mountain, He will swallow up the covering*
> *which is over all peoples,*
> *Even the veil which is stretched over all nations.*
> *He will swallow up death for all time,*
> *And the Lord GOD will wipe tears away from all faces,*
> *And He will remove the reproach of His people from all*
> *the earth . . .*
>
> (Isaiah 25:7–8)

God's heart is to restore His order and His healing to this very damaged world.

A suggestion for what to say:

> Under the authority of Jesus, I claim freedom from the enemy's covering of lies. I declare that Satan's rights, in this area of my life, finish today. In Christ Jesus I am in a sheltered place of truth and light. In Jesus' name I address the powers of darkness _____ [name spirits such as those promoting deception, fear, unbelief, rejection, infirmity, shame, being orphaned] and command you to leave now from every part of my being.

8. Healing for body, soul and spirit

The title of this book is *God's Covering – A Place of Healing*. The Good Samaritan took the injured traveler to a safe dwelling place for the fullness of his healing. The side of the road was far too exposed and dangerous a place in which to restore the health of this needy individual. Birds drowning in an oil spill at sea are cleaned up only when they have been taken out of the oil and into a special sanctuary.

We have seen through the writing of the prophet Ezekiel that this is how God has always planned to restore His people: by renewing His covering, re-establishing His covenant and administering His cleansing and healing:

> *"Then I [the Lord] passed by you and saw you, and behold, you were at the time for love; so I spread My skirt over you and covered your*

nakedness. I also swore [made a oath] to you and entered into a covenant with you so that you became Mine," declares the Lord GOD. *"Then I bathed you with water, washed off your blood from you and anointed you with oil."*

(Ezekiel 16:8–9)

It is time to receive His cleansing water and His healing oil.

A suggestion for what to say:

Father God, You have renewed Your covering and Your covenant with me through Jesus, my Lord. As I receive Your Holy Spirit in the wounded places of my life, I ask for the fullness of Your order and Your healing in my spirit, soul and body. My life got distorted and damaged when I was caught outside the sheltered place of Your presence. Thank You for Your cleansing and healing, in Jesus' precious name.

9. The re-covering of land, homes and places of worship

The ground which God has given to mankind at creation has been defiled and cursed because of our disobedience. God told Adam,

"Because you have listened to the voice of your wife, and have eaten from the tree about which I commanded you, saying, 'You shall not eat from it': cursed is the ground because of you; in toil you will eat of it all the days of your life."

(Genesis 3:17)

Land and buildings are increasingly defiled by the sinfulness of those occupying the ground. Those occupants in turn suffer the consequence of that defilement, as Leviticus 18:24–25 makes clear:

"Do not defile yourselves by any of these things; for by all of these the nations which I am casting out before you have become defiled. For the land has become defiled, therefore I have brought its punishment upon it, so the land has spewed out its inhabitants."

The good news is that ground and buildings can be reclaimed to be a place of blessing, safety and fruitfulness, when those rightfully occupying the ground walk according to God's order and under His covering. A sound umbrella which protects people, does the same for the ground they are standing on. God promises that, when His people turn back to Him and seek forgiveness, He will heal their land:

"If . . . My people, who are called by My name humble themselves and pray and seek My face and turn from their wicked ways, then I will hear from heaven, will forgive their sin and will heal their land."

(2 Chronicles 7:13–14)

A suggestion for what to say:

Father God, I/we bring before You this home/this land/this church, for which I/we have rightful responsibility. We confess the sin of ourselves and those who have been here before us. We forgive those who have defiled this ground and brought spiritual disorder into this place. As we receive Your forgiveness and Your cleansing through Jesus our Lord, we ask that the godly covering, blessing and fruitfulness of this place would be restored.

Under the authority of Jesus, I/we expel all the powers of darkness, which have had rights to defile this place.

Last words

Since the fall of Adam and Eve, God has given instructions to man. They are given so that we can keep right with the spiritual law and order of the universe, and know His covering. The world, or rather the ruler of the world, tells us that God's order is old-fashioned, restrictive and contrary to our rights as a human being. The more that the enemy can undermine the knowledge of God's ways of covering, the more we become spiritually exposed to the control of the powers of darkness. Respect for God's law and order, right authority, godly leadership, marriage and parenting is absent, or fast deteriorating, in many cultures.

God has a rescue plan for a world seriously exposed to spiritual darkness. Saving lives is nearly always costly. For Jesus it was agony, but as we respond in confession of our own sin and forgiveness of those who have damaged our lives, He delights in restoring God's covering to the places where we have been out of His shelter. We can be released from the captivity of the enemy and find healing and blessing in the covenant relationship which God has made with His people, through faith in Jesus Christ.

Jesus taught His disciples the key issues to speak out to their Heavenly Father:

> *'Pray, then, in this way:*
> *"Our Father who is in heaven,*
> *Hallowed be Your name.*
> *Your kingdom come.*
> *Your will be done,*
> *On earth as it is in heaven.*
> *Give us this day our daily bread.*
> *And forgive us our debts, as we also have forgiven our debtors.*
> *And do not lead us into temptation, but deliver us from [the]*
> *   evil [one].'"*
>
> (Matthew 6:9–13)

When God's covering is reinstated in any part of our lives, it *is* the change of kingdoms which Jesus has instructed us to seek. When the dark place is filled with light, it *is* the deliverance which He has encouraged us to pursue. When healing comes to the exposed and damaged places in our lives, it *is* the life-giving food which He has taught us to request. In order to maintain right order in all our relationships, God's instruction to forgive *is* the only way to walk.

God's covering is not just an end in itself. It is the divine shelter which dismisses the enemy's hostility and lies. It gives the opportunity for a deeper individual and corporate relationship with Jesus and for true healing from all the damage caused by spiritual exposure. A bandage over torn flesh is not itself the healing, but it shields the wound from germs and allows the repair to be completed. The Good Samaritan first bandaged the wounds of the traumatized traveler and then he poured oil and wine over the wounded place to promote the healing. He also took him to a safe dwelling place where the restoration could be completed.

Because of God's commitment to His covenant with His people, Jesus is watching out for wounded travelers, like you and me, to reveal where some part of us has been left by the roadside. With the help of His disciples, He wants to re-cover us from any places of exposure and to pour out His wonderful healing. To be more under godly covering is very simply to be more *in Christ*. In Him, we can then receive the flow of abundant life which is actually Jesus Himself living *in us* by His Spirit.

Let's help one another to be open to God's precious re-covery service.

Anger is the most powerful of emotions. It can be the driving force that enables us to achieve the seemingly impossible or the stumbling block that traps us into a life style characterized by unforgiveness, bitterness, broken relationships and violence. Keys presented in this book will explain how you can deal with the accumulation of anger from past events and how you can in future deal with the situations that cause you to feel angry. The book also provides much needed understanding for those in the caring ministries who are seeking to help those with 'an anger problem'.

Anger: How Do You Handle It? *by Paul & Liz Giffin*
£6.99 | 978-185240-4505 | 112pp | Sovereign World Ltd

Whilst the Church's standards in sexual matters may be higher than those of the world they are often still nowhere near God's standards. We live in a world that has distorted the godly concept of sexuality. As a result there are many Christians living in guilt or struggling because of a lack of knowledge, wrong past choices or as a consequence of sins that others have committed against them. The driving force behind the ungodly expression of our sexuality is a seeking after false love and acceptance. The author brilliantly exposes the lies of the enemy, which can trap us into ungodly sexual practices.

Sex: God's Truth *by Jill Southern*
£6.99 | 978-185240-4529 | 128pp | Sovereign World Ltd

When we realize that relationships are more than just a physical meeting of two people, we begin to understand that some of our relationships might have affected our lives in a negative way. We may find ourselves damaged and tied in a place of bondage from which God wants us to be set free. A way of describing this unseen hold that ties us to bad relationships is an ungodly soul-tie. It is a tie in the spiritual realm that has a hold on the soul. As you read this book you will discover how to find release from ungody soul-ties and most impotantly experience God's freedom and healing.

Soul Ties: The Unseen Bond in Relationships *by David Cross*
£6.99 | 978-185240-4512 | 128pp | Sovereign World Ltd

Many Christians carry the scars of their experiences of physical, verbal, racial, emotional, spiritual or sexual abuse. As a consequence their life is controlled by confusion and shame, and they go through life feeling rejected and fearful of further rejection. For many, death can even become a preferable option to a life without hope. They have experiences which they are trying to forget or don't want to talk about but which, nevertheless, still influence their lives and hold them back from living the abundant life that Jesus came to bring.

Hope & Healing for the Abused *by Paul & Liz Griffin*
£7.99 | 978-185240-4802 | 128pp | Sovereign World Ltd

Frida witnessed her family being massacred by Hutu men with machetes and was then asked how she wanted to die. She could not afford a bullet, which they offered to sell her, so instead received what should have been a fatal blow to the head. She was put in a mass grave with her slaughtered family only to find herself still alive and conscious. She eventually climbed out of the pit covered in filth and blood. Remarkably, Frida's message is one of immense hope and personal deliverance pointing towards the transforming power of forgiveness. This book tells the true, dramatic story of life amid the horror of genocide and her miraculous escape.

Frida: Chosen to Die, Destined to Live *by Frida Gashumba*
£8.99 | 978-185240-4758 | 176pp | Sovereign World Ltd

Sovereign World Ltd
&
Ellel Ministries International

In a stroke of divine master planning both Sovereign World and Ellel Ministries were independently founded in the same year – 1986.

Sovereign World, founded by Chris Mungeam, has become a widely respected Christian publishing imprint and Ellel Ministries, founded by Peter Horrobin, has developed a worldwide network of Centres, each designed to resource and equip the Church through healing retreats, courses and training schools.

Twenty years later, in April 2006, Ellel Ministries purchased Sovereign World Ltd to continue the precious work of publishing outstanding Christian teaching, as well as to create a publishing arm for Ellel Ministries. It was a divine knitting together of these two organizations both of which share the vision to proclaim the Kingdom of God by preaching the good news, healing the broken-hearted and setting the captives free.

If you would like to know more about Ellel Ministries their UK contact information is:

International Headquarters
Ellel Grange
Ellel
Lancaster
LA2 0HN
UK

Tel: +44 (0)1524 751651
Fax: +44 (0)1524 751738
Email: info.grange@ellelministries.org

For details of other Centres please refer to the website at:
www.ellelministries.org